JUMBO JACK'S COOKBOOKS

AUDUBON MEDIA CORPORATION
301 BROADWAY • AUDUBON IA 50025
1-800-798-2635

DIAL - A - DREAM
COOKBOOK

by

Bruce Carlson

* * * * * * * * *

**QUIXOTE
PRESS
31798 K18S
Sioux City, IA
51109**
800-571-BOOK
PRINTED IN U.S.A.

3

DEDICATION

-to the Research Staff
who did all the interviews
and all the statistical work
for this book.

TABLE OF CONTENTS

Recipes for dishes to promote dreams of

FLIGHT

ROMANCE

POWER

CHILDHOOD

The recipes in this cookbook are those that have been shown to promote pleasant dreams rather than unpleasant ones. This is because only the oddest among us would want to promote bad dreams.

The reader might be alerted to a couple of things to avoid in order to discourage bad dreams. These are:

(1) combinations of sweet and tart foods
(2) highly spiced foods
(3) foods extremely high in water content like watermelons
(4) raw fruits and veggies with highly adhering skins such as pears or apples

Our research has revealed that pleasant dreams tend to be ones that fall within one of the following five types

(1) Flight . . . travel . . . movement
(2) Romance
(3) Power . . . influence . . . wealth
(4) Incidents from your childhood

This cookbook is organized along those types of dreams and it lists recipes that tend to result in those kinds of dreams.

These recipes are therefore organized by type of dream desired and type of dish.

PREFACE

Dreams don't have to "just happen". You can partly determine what and how you dream by what you eat before going to bed.

So, Mom was right . . . well partly right when she warned you not to eat this or that at bed time . . . for fear it'd give you bad dreams. Some foods will do just that.

Starting with this cookbook and some experimentation with your own responses to various foods, you can . . .

Dial Your Dreams!

FOREWORD

Bruce Carlson has asked me to say something nice about this book here on this page.

I'd do that too, if he'd ever pay me for the last time I said something nice about one of his books.

My personal opinion is that he's either been snifing the pickling spice or taking little naps in the kitchen with his head bone too close to the microwave.

Prof. Phil Hey
Briar Cliff College
Sioux City, IA

FLIGHT

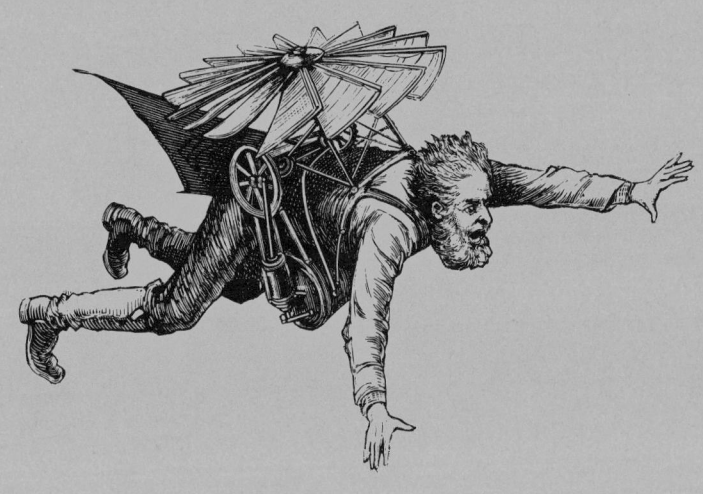

APPETIZERS

&

BEVERAGES

PARTY MIX

¾ C. oil
1 pkg. Lipton onion & California dip
3 C. honey cut Cherrios

3 C. Corn Chexs
Garlic salt
Nuts

Mix oil, Lipton onion and California dip. Stir well, then add Cherrios and Corn Chexs. Stir well, coating breakfast food. Salt real good and put on cookie sheet and put in oven at 250° for 40 minutes. Stir occasionally. Then add nuts

CHEESE BALL

½ lb. American cheese
¼ lb. Cheddar cheese
2 oz. blue cheese
2 tsp. Worcestershire sauce

½ C. mayonnaise
1 T. chopped onion
1 T. pickle relish

Melt cheese in double boiler. Cool to nearly room temperature and add mayonnaise, onion, relish and Worcestershire sauce and blend. Chill at least six hours. Shape into balls and roll into nuts.

CHEESE LOG

½ lb. Cheddar cheese, shredded
4 oz. cream cheese, softened

1 tsp. garlic salt

Combine all ingredients and form into a log. Sprinkle with chili powder until well coated. Chill and serve with crackers.

17

VEGETABLE DIP

1 carton (cup) sour cream
1 C. real mayonnaise
2 T. parsley flakes

2 T. dill
2 T. minced onion
½ tsp. celery salt

Cream all together and chill. Serve as a dip for raw vegetables.

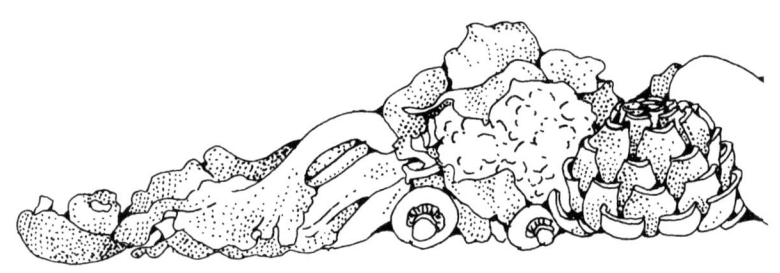

DILL DIP

12 oz. sour cream
1-1½ C. real mayonnaise
2 tsp. parsley flakes
Dried green onions

1 T. + 1 tsp. beau monde
1 T. + 1 tsp. minced onion
1 T. + 1 tsp. dill seed
1 T. creamy horseradish (optional)

Mix all together and serve with raw vegetables.

CREAMY BEEF DIP

1 pkg. (3 oz.) dried chipped beef
2 tsp. vinegar
1 tsp. Worcestershire sauce
1 pkg. (8 oz.) cream cheese

½ tsp. onion or garlic powder
½ C. mayonnaise
¼ C. chopped green pepper (opt.)

Tear or cut beef into small pieces. Combine all ingredients and mix well. Heat in small glass or ceramic casserole in oven or microwave until hot, (3 or 4 minutes in microwave) or about 12 minutes in oven. Serve hot as a dip for vegetables or chips or chill and use as a spread for crackers.

18

HOLIDAY CIDER

6 sticks cinnamon
16 cloves, cut up
1 tsp. whole allspice
2 orange slices

6 C. apple juice or cider
2 C. cranberry juice cocktail
4 C. sugar

Put cinnamon, cloves and allspice in bag. Simmer all ten minutes. Take out bag and oranges. Add 1 C. rum (optional). Pour over round peppermint candy in a cup and serve hot.

MULLED CIDER PUNCH (10 Cups)

2 qt. apple cider or juice
1 C. apricot nectar
1 C. orange juice

½ tsp. cinnamon
Orange slices

In saucepan, combine cider, nectar, orange juice and cinnamon; heat and stir. Garnish with orange slices.

CHOCOLATE (SYRUP) MINI-MIX FOR MILK DRINK

1 C. cocoa
2 C. sugar
¼ tsp. salt

2 C. water
2 T. vanilla

Combine cocoa, sugar and salt in pan. Slowly stir water in and simmer until smooth and thick, about 5 minutes, stirring constantly. Remove from heat and cool. Add vanilla. Store covered in refrigerator. Will keep several days. Makes 3 cups.

CHEESE SPREAD

½ lb. American cheese
½ lb. Velveeta cheese
½ lb. Colby cheese
Grate cheeses altogether
1 4-oz. jar chopped pimento

1 dash Accent
1 T. sugar
1 pt. mayonnaise
1 T. mustard

Mix rest of ingredients together with cheese. Add garlic salt and onion if desired.

CHEESE HAM SPREAD

8 oz. pkg. softened cream cheese
1½ C. shredded Cheddar cheese
Blend all until smooth.

¼ C. salad dressing

¼ C. chopped onion
1 tsp. Worcestershire sauce
1 tsp. paprika

Dash of salt
¾ C. shredded ham

Serve on crackers or use for stuffing celery.

HOT CHEESE SPREAD

8 oz. pkg. cream cheese
2 T. milk
2½ oz. chipped beef, cut fine
¼ C. chopped green pepper
2 T. dried onion

½ tsp. garlic salt
1 C. sour cream
½ C. pecans
2 T. butter
¼ tsp. salt

Mix cream cheese, milk, beef, pepper, onion, garlic and sour cream and put in flat pan. Heat pecans, butter and salt and put on top of cheese mixture. Bake at 350° for 20 minutes. Dip crackers or potato chips into mix.

CANDY

&

COOKIES

CHERRY NUT BARS

2¼ C. sifted flour
½ C. sugar
1 C. butter
2 eggs, plus 1 egg yolk
1½ C. brown sugar

1½ tsp. baking powder
½ tsp. salt, sifted with ¼ C. flour
½ C. maraschino cherries
½ C. nuts

Mix flour, ½ C. sugar and butter. Spread in 9 x 13-inch pan. Bake 12 minutes at 350°. Mix eggs and yolk, brown sugar, baking powder, salt and ¼ C. flour, cherries and nuts. Spread over crust and bake 20 minutes.

FROSTING:
1 egg white
2 C. powdered sugar

2 T. cherry juice

Mix together and spread on cooled bars.

BANANA-NUT COOKIES

1½ C. sifted flour
1 C. sugar
½ tsp. soda
1 tsp. salt
¼ tsp. nutmeg
¾ tsp. cinnamon

¾ C. shortening
1 egg (well beaten)
1 C. mashed fully ripe bananas
1¾ C. quick oatmeal
½ C. chopped nuts

Sift dry ingredients. Cut in shortening. Add egg, bananas and oatmeal. Beat until blended. Bake on ungreased pan at 400° for about 15 minutes. Remove from pan immediately.

PEANUT BLOSSOMS

1¾ C. flour
1 tsp. soda
½ tsp. salt
¾ C. oleo
¼ C. peanut butter

½ C. sugar
½ C. brown sugar
1 egg
2 T. milk
1 tsp. vanilla

Sift together flour, soda and salt. Cream oleo, peanut butter and sugars. Add egg, milk and vanilla. Add dry ingredients and cream together. Shape batter into small balls and roll in white sugar. Place on ungreased cookie sheet. Bake at 375° for 8 minutes. Remove from oven and press chocolate star in the center of each cookie. Bake again 2 to 5 minutes.

Meisenbach.

BUTTERSCOTCH CHIP OATMEAL COOKIES

1 C. brown sugar
1 C. white sugar
1 C. shortening
2 eggs
1 tsp. soda

Vanilla
2 C. flour
2 C. rolled oats
1 pkg. chips

Cream shortening and sugar. Add eggs and vanilla; beat. Add dry ingredients and chips. Mix well. Bake at 350° for 10-15 minutes.

BREADS

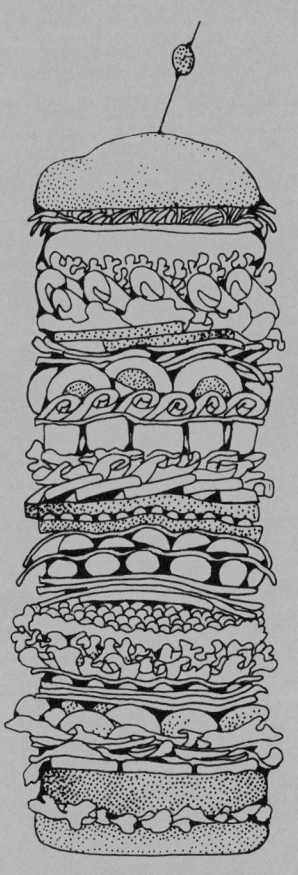

KOLACHES

1 pkg. reg. vanilla pudding
½ C. butter
½ C. warm water
2 tsp. salt
Fruit pie filling mix

1½ C. milk
2 pkg. yeast
2 eggs
5 C. flour

Cook pudding with milk. Add butter and cool. Dissolve yeast in warm water. Add to yeast, eggs, salt and cooled pudding mixture. Add flour and mix into dough. Knead and let rise to double in bulk. Punch down and form into small balls. Push down center of each ball (tart like center) and fill with favorite pie filling mix (I use cherry). Let rise on greased cookie sheet. Bake at 350° for 15 minutes. Cool and glaze with mixture of powdered sugar and remaining pie filling juice. Makes 3 to 4 dozen.

DOUGH FOR DANISH SWEET ROLLS OR RAISED DOUGHNUTS

1 C. very warm milk
¼ C. lard
1 cake yeast
1 tsp. sugar
Flour

¼ C. sugar
1 tsp. salt
½ C. warm water
1 egg

Dissolve yeast in warm water; set aside. Mix milk, sugar, lard, salt and add 2 C. flour. Add yeast mixture. Add more flour until dough feels about right. Raise dough once, make out into sweet rolls or doughnuts, raise once more and bake rolls at 375° for 20 minutes.

CARAMEL ROLLS

2½ C. warm water   1 pkg. yellow cake mix
2 pkg. yeast   1 tsp. salt
5-5½ C. flour

TOPPING:
2 C. brown sugar   2 sticks oleo
6 tsp. water

    Dissolve yeast in water; add cake mix and salt. Mix well and add flour and let rise until double. No kneading is necessary. When doubled divide in half. Roll out each half and spread with butter, sprinkle with sugar and cinnamon. Roll each half and cut into 12 rolls. Place in two 9 x 13-inch pans in which you have divided the topping. Let rise until double. Bake at 350° for 20 minutes. Makes 24 rolls. To make topping, combine ingredients and bring to boil. Divide into two pans and let cool a little before placing rolls on top.

SOUDOUGH STARTER

1 pkg. dry yeast   2½ C. warm water
1 T. sugar   2 C. flour

    Dissolve yeast in ½ cup warm water. Stir in remaining water, sugar and flour. Beat all smooth and cover. Let stand 5-10 days, stirring 2 or 3 times a day. Cover and refrigerate till ready to use. To keep starter going; add ¾ C. flour and 1 tsp. sugar after some is used. If not all used within 10 days, add 1 tsp. sugar. Bread, rolls, carrot cake, pancakes, coffee cakes, etc. may be made using this starter.

HAWAIIAN SWEET BREAD WITH DILL DIP

1 pkg. dry yeast
1 C. milk
½ C. butter or oleo
4 eggs

½ C. warm water
1 C. sugar
½ tsp. salt
4½ C. flour (approx.)

½ pt. Hellman's mayonnaise
1 tsp. dill weed
1 tsp. onion, chopped fine

½ pt. sour cream
1 tsp. Lawry's seasoned salt

Dissolve yeast in warm water. Mix ingredients well and set aside to rise in greased bowl. After rising, knead and form into 2 round loaves. Use pie pans or round cake pans. Bake at 350° for 40-50 minutes. For 1 loaf, cut off top and scoop out ½ of insides, making a shell. Tear off bread you scooped out. Break into chunks. Pour dip into shell and dip chunks in dip.

BROWN BREAD

1½ C. sugar, (brown & white, mixed)
1 tsp. soda
1½ C. dark molasses
4 C. sour milk (part water if desired)
2 eggs

2½ C. graham or whole wheat flour
1 tsp. salt
1 C. white flour
4 tsp. baking powder

29

AMERICAN INDIAN FRY BREAD

6 C. warm water   2 T. yeast
¼-1 C. sugar or honey   2 T. salt
Flour - white or wheat

Let rise 10-15 minutes at least. Flatten a small pingpong ball sized piece of dough and poke a hole in the center. Fry immediately in at least 1 inch hot grease. Turn and remove when both sides are golden brown.

ROLLS

2 C. warm water   2 pkg. dry yeast
½ C. sugar   2 tsp. salt
1 egg   ¼ C. melted shortening
6½-7 C. flour

Dissolve yeast in water; add sugar, salt, half of the flour. Beat well 2 minutes. Add eggs and oil; knead well. Let rise double; make out in 1'' rolls. Let rise until double in size. Bake at 325° for 25 minutes.

3 HOUR ROLLS

1 cake yeast   ¼ C. lukewarm water
1 C. scalded milk   2 T. lard
2 T. sugar   1 egg
1 tsp. salt   3½ C. flour

Dissolve yeast in lukewarm water. To milk, add lard and sugar. Cool, then add the yeast mixture and beaten egg. Add salt and flour. Mix and cover and let rise till double. Then make into rolls and double again. Bake at 350° for about 30 minutes.

VEGGIES

CUCUMBERS FOR COMPANY

2 medium cucumbers
1 20-oz. can pineapple tidbits,
  (drained)
½ C. sour cream

½ C. whipped cream
1 T. salt
2 T. chopped fresh dill or
  1 tsp. dried dill weed

    Peel and dice cucumbers; add well drained pineapple and remaining ingredients, blending well. Sweeten a bit if desired. Refrigerate at least 4 hours before serving. Serves 6 to 8.

GOURMET POTATOES

6-8 long potatoes
¼ C. butter
½ C. dairy sour cream
½ tsp. pepper

2 C. grated Cheddar cheese
⅓ C. chopped green onion
1 tsp. salt

    Boil potatoes with skins on. When cooked, cool, peel and grate. Melt together cheese and butter. Stir in onion, sour cream, salt and pepper. Combine cheese mixture with potatoes. Pour into greased casserole. Dot with 2 T. butter and sprinkle with paprika. Bake 30-35 minutes at 350°.

ORANGE SWEET POTATO CASSEROLE (Serves 6)

⅓ C. sugar
⅓ C. brown sugar
⅔ C. orange juice

1 T. grated orange rind
2 T. butter
4 large sweet potatoes

    Cook and quarter the sweet potatoes. Layer in baking dish and dot with butter. Combine remaining ingredients and pour over potatoes. Bake 1 hour in a 300° oven. Baste potatoes occasionally with sauce while they are baking. A ''prepare ahead'' casserole, if the potatoes darken upon standing, the orange juice will restore the color as they bake. Slip in the oven 1 hour before serving.

FRIED ZUCCHINI CAKES

2 C. zucchini, grated
½ C. onion, grated
2 T. sugar
2 T. cornmeal
1 tsp. salt
1 C. flour
½ C. milk

    Mix together and drop into hot grease. Fry until golden brown.

CHEESEY VEGETABLES

2 sacks frozen mixed vegetables
1 can cream of mushroom soup
1 jar Cheez Whiz
Bread crumbs, potato chips or
crushed corn flakes (whichever
you prefer)

    Cook vegetables and drain. Mix Cheez Whiz and mushroom soup and pour over vegetables. Top with bread crumbs and bake 20 to 30 minutes in 350° oven.
    Variation: Use 1 can cheese soup in place of the mushroom soup and Cheez Whiz. An onion may be chopped and cooked with vegetables. Use 1 C. Velveeta cheese, ¼ C. canned milk, and 1 can cream of celery soup mixed with vegetables.

MARINATED ONION RINGS

½ C. vinegar
½ C. corn oil
1 C. catsup
Sliced onions

    Combine vinegar, oil and catsup in a quart jar and shake well. Then add the sliced onions and refrigerate overnight. When the onions are gone, slice more and add to the jar. Especially good for picnics or cook-outs.

CARROT CASSEROLE

4 C. carrots, sliced round
¼ C. flour
½ tsp. salt & dash of pepper
2 C. milk
1 can French fried onion
¼ C. melted butter
Dash Worcestershire sauce
1 C. Velveeta cheese

Cook carrots. Make sauce with flour, butter, seasoning, milk and cheese. Cook until creamy. Layer carrots, sauce and onion rings in a casserole. Bake 30 minutes at 350°.

FOOLPROOF CORN CUSTARD

1 10-oz. can mushroom soup
1 5-oz. can evaporated milk
2 eggs, slightly beaten
1 12-oz. can whole kernel corn, drained or
   use cream style (I use 1 pt. home canned)
⅓ C. toasted bread crumbs
2 T. flour
¼ tsp. salt
¼ tsp. pepper
1 T. melted butter

Blend soup, milk and eggs and stir well. Stir in flour and seasonings. Gently stir in corn. Turn into a greased 8 x 8-inch shallow pan. Toss bread crumbs with melted butter and sprinkle over top. Bake at 350° for 40 to 45 minutes or until knife inserted in center comes out clean.

BROCCOLI CASSEROLE (Serves 8)

3 green onions, chopped (tops & all)
2 stalks celery, chopped (tops & all)
1 can cream of mushroom soup
1 roll garlic cheese

2 4-oz. cans mushrooms
3 pkg. (frozen) chopped broccoli
Ritz crackers
Butter

Saute onions and celery in butter in large skillet. Add mushroom soup, cheese and mushrooms. Heat until cheese is melted. Cook broccoli and drain. Mix with the sauce in skillet and put in buttered casserole. Top with crumbled Ritz crackers and dabs of butter. Bake at 350° for 20 to 30 minutes until bubbly. Can be made ahead and stored in refrigerator or frozen.

PICKLED CHINESE BEETS

3 (No. 303) cans beets
   (drain & save juice)
1 C. sugar
1 C. regular vinegar
2 T. cornstarch
24 whole cloves

3 T. catsup
3 T. cooking oil
Dash of salt
1 tsp. vanilla
1½ C. beet juice

Mix the cornstarch with the sugar, then add remainder of ingredients, except the drained beets, and cook over medium heat until mixture thickens. About 3 minutes. Cool, then add beets and refrigerate indefinately.

SOUPS

&

SANDWICHES

HAMBURGER VEGETABLE SOUP

1½ lb. ground beef
1 medium onion
2 C. tomato juice
1 C. sliced carrots
⅓ C. flour
1 tsp. salt

1/8 tsp. pepper
1 tsp. seasoned salt
1-2 C. diced potatoes
4 C. milk
1 can tomato soup

Brown ground beef and onion in large pan. Stir in tomato juice, carrots and seasonings. Cover and cook over low heat until carrots are almost tender. Add potatoes and cook until tender. Combine flour with 1 C. milk, stir into soup. Add remaining milk. Heat to boiling, stirring to prevent sticking. Add can of soup and stir in. Heat a few more minutes. The can of tomato soup is optional, but it adds flavor. Serves 8-12.

PORK BURGERS

3 lb. pork
¾ tsp. Accent
1 scant tsp. salt
1 scant tsp. black pepper

1 scant tsp. white pepper
3 T. Worcestershire sauce
3 T. soy sauce

This can all be varied a little, depending on your family's taste. It is nice to mix the pork burger mixture a few hours before you intend to cook it, in order to let all of the seasonings marinate. Shape porkburgers into ¼ lb. patties and fry or grill on a charcoal grill. They are especially tasty when charcoaled. These patties freeze well and it is really hand to have some made ahead in the freezer. Note: When cooking on a charcoal grill, we like to brush each side with a B-B-Q sauce the last 2 or 3 minutes of cooking time.

BEEF BURGERS

1 lb. ground beef	1 tsp. salt
¾ C. catsup	1 T. prepared mustard
1 tsp. sugar	Scant tsp. vinegar

Simmer for 25 minutes. Add pepper and onion if desired.

NO PEEK STEW

2½ lb. stew meat	1 can whole tomatoes
1 small onion	2 T. vinegar
2 large potatoes	1 T. Worcestershire sauce
3 carrots	1 tsp. horseradish
3 stalks celery	1 tsp. garlic salt
1 can tomato soup	1 tsp. pepper

Mix soup, tomatoes, vinegar and seasonings. Use a Dutch oven. Layer all other ingredients and pour liquid mixture on top. Bake at 275° for 5 hours. Don't peek.

HAMBURGER ROLL-UPS

2 lb. ground beef	3 T. catsup
10 slices bacon	2 tsp. Worcestershire sauce
¼ C. onion, minced	1½ tsp. salt
1 egg, beaten	½ tsp. pepper
1 C. cheese, grated	

Mix all ingredients except bacon. Make into 10 patties. Roll the edge of each in a slice of bacon and fasten with toothpicks. Broil on both sides until desired doneness (about 8 minutes on each side). Serves 10.

SALADS

SAUERKRAUT SALAD

2 C. chopped sauerkraut, drained
½ C. sugar
½ C. thinly sliced celery
½ green pepper (cut in thin strips)

½ C. grated carrots
½ C. chopped onions
Sm. jar chopped pimento, drained

Combine kraut and sugar, mixing well. Let stand 30 minutes. Add remaining ingredients, stir well. Cover and chill for at least 12 hours.

SPINACH SALAD

2 pkg. frozen chopped spinach
   (thawed & drained)
½ C. chopped onion

½ C. chopped celery
1 C. grated sharp Cheddar cheese
3 hard boiled eggs, diced

Thaw and drain spinach by squeezing well. Mix spinach, onion, celery, cheese and eggs.

DRESSING:
1 to 1¼ C. mayonnaise
½ tsp. Tabasco sauce

½ tsp. salt
2 tsp. horseradish

Combine dressing ingredients and mix with vegetable mixture and chill.

TEXAS FRENCH DRESSING

1 can tomato soup
1 C. salad oil
½ C. sugar
¾ C. cider vinegar
1 tsp. scant pepper

1 clove garlic
1 large onion, grated
3 tsp. prepared mustard
1 tsp. Worcestershire sauce
1 tsp. salt

Combine in quart jar and shake vigorously.

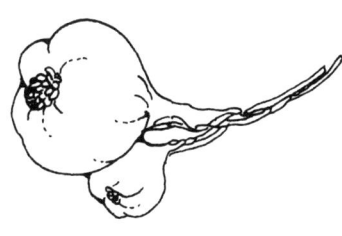

FRESH VEGETABLE SALAD

Uncooked cauliflower, broccoli, carrots,   Hidden Valley ranch dressing mix
    onions & cucumber   1 C. sour cream
    Cut vegetables into bite sized pieces. Prepare Hidden Valley Ranch dressing.
Add 1 C. sour cream. Mix dressing with vegetables and chill.

SOUR CREAM DRESSING

1 C. sour cream   ½ tsp. salt
1 tsp. lemon juice   1 tsp. chives
¼ tsp. honey   1/8 tsp. paprika
1 tsp. powdered horseradish   1 tsp. dry mustard
    For variety, chop 2 hard cooked eggs into dressing. Can also use clove of garlic,
crushed.

MOSTACCIOLI SALAD

1 lb. mostaccioli noodles   2½ tsp. diced garlic
2 C. vinegar   ½ C. red pepper (diced)
2 C. sugar   2½ tsp. Accent
1 cucumber (diced)   3 T. plus ½ tsp. parsley flakes
1 onion (diced)   3 T. plus ½ tsp. prepared mustard
2½ tsp. coarse ground pepper   2½ tsp. salt
    Cook noodles in boiling water in which you've added 1 tsp. salt and 1/8 C. oil.
Cook vinegar and sugar until dissolved clear and cool. Mix vegetables and seasonings. Then mix all ingredients and stir. Let set overnight.

MIXED VEGETABLE SALAD

1 pkg. frozen mixed vegetables
   (salted, cooked, cooled & drained)
1 can red or kidney beans, drained

½ green pepper, chopped
½ to 1 C. celery, chopped
1 chopped onion, optional

DRESSING:
½ to 1 C. vinegar
1 C. sugar

1 T. dry mustard
1 T. flour (heaping)

   Bring dressing ingredients to a boil and cool. When vegetables and dressing are cool, mix together and marinate overnight.

CUCUMBER SALAD

1 pkg. lime Jello
1 C. boiling water
2 tsp. lemon juice
1½ C. crushed pineapple

½ C. salad dressing
1 C. ground cucumber
   (peeled & seeded)
½ tsp. salt

   Mix Jello, water and lemon juice. Let stand till cool and partially set. Whip till thick and foamy, beat in salad dressing. Before adding cucumber, be sure it is well drained. Squeeze till liquid is all gone. Add the cucumber, onion, salt and pineapple and stir. Let set in refrigerator.

SUMMER SALAD

1 small can crushed pineapple
½ C. sugar
1 pkg. orange Jello
1 scant C. hot water

1 C. nuts
1 C. grated cheese
1 C. Dream Whip
Dash lemon juice

   Heat pineapple and sugar, then add Jello with water. Refrigerate until partially set. Add nuts, cheese and fold in Dream Whip and lemon juice.

CAULIFLOWER-BROCCOLI SALAD

1 med. head cauliflower (cut in sm. flowers)
3 med. stalks broccoli (cut in bite size pieces)
2 sm. bunches green onions
  (chopped greens too)
1 C. mayonnaise

1 T. sugar
1 T. vinegar
½ C. sour cream
Dash Worcestershire sauce
Dash of Tabasco

    Pour dressing mixture over vegetables and refrigerate. Should be made 24 hours before serving. Will keep several days.

24 HOUR LETTUCE SALAD

1 head lettuce, break up
½ C. diced celery
½ C. diced green pepper

1 10-oz. box partially frozen peas
1 small red onion, sliced

    Put in order in a 9 x 13-inch pan. Frost with 2 cups Miracle Whip. Sprinkle 4 oz. pkg. of shredded cheese and 8 sliced fried bacon. Chill overnight.

CARROT PICKLES

2 lb. carrots, boiled til tender
1 sliced & chopped onion
1 green pepper
1 C. sugar
1 C. tomato soup

¾ C. vinegar
½ C. Mazola oil
1 tsp. salt
1 tsp. mustard
1 tsp. pepper

    Heat to boiling point sugar, tomato soup, vinegar, oil, salt, mustard and pepper. Drain carrots and add to dressing, plus onion and pepper. Keeps in refrigerator indefinetely.

TASTY TACO SALAD

1 lb. lean ground pork
1 can (8 oz.) cut-up tomatoes
¼ C. chopped onion
2-3 tsp. chili powder
¼ tsp. garlic powder

Salt & pepper
1 head lettuce
2 tomatoes (cut in wedges)
¼ C. (1 oz.) shredded Cheddar
cheese

In 9'' skillet, brown ground pork over moderate heat and drain. Stir in undrained canned tomatoes, onion, chili powder and garlic powder. Bring to boiling. Reduce heat and simmer, uncovered until most liquid evaporates (about 15 minutes), stirring occasionally. Season to taste with salt and pepper. Line four salad bowls with lettuce leaves; tear remaining lettuce into bite-sized pieces. Divide among the four bowls. Place ½ C. pork mixture on lettuce. Arrange tomato wedges on top of salad. Sprinkle with cheese and crushed corn chips. Serves 4.

YOGURT SALAD

2 3-oz. boxes Jello (any flavor)
2 C. hot water

Cool Whip (medium size)
2 containers yogurt (flavor as Jello)

Mix Jello and hot water together and add 6-8 ice cubes. Let set in refrigerator until partially congealed. Fold in yogurt. Then fold in Cool Whip. Fruit may be added if desired.

DELICIOUS SALAD

½ C. sugar
1 rounded T. flour
1 egg
1 #2 can pineapple chunks
1 T. butter

1 C. heavy cream (whipped)
3 bananas, diced
1 C. nuts
¼ lb. small marshmallows

Combine sugar and flour. Stir into beaten egg. Add juice, drained from pineapple and the butter. Cook in double boiler or over very low heat until thickened and smooth. Stir all the time this is cooking. Cool then add rest of ingredients.

PINE-COT SALAD

2 pkg. orange Jello
1 tall can chunk or crushed pineapple (drain)

1 No. 2 can apricots (drain & mash)
1½ C. small marshmallows

DRESSING:
½ C. sugar
2 T. flour
1 C. reserved juice

1 egg, beaten
1 C. whipped cream

Reserve 1 C. juice from both fruits for dressing. Make Jello as usual using remaining juice as part of liquid. Add fruit and spread marshmallows on top. Pour into 9 x 13-inch pan. Cover with dressing when set. For dressing: Mix together and cook till thick. Let cool and add 1 C. whipped cream. Spread over top of Jello.

CRANBERRY SALAD

1 qt. cranberries
2 C. sugar
1 pkg. raspberry Jello
1 C. raw apple, diced

1 C. water
15 large marshmallows
1 C. celery, diced
½ C. pecans

Boil cranberries, sugar and water until berries are soft. While hot, stir in marshmallows and Jello. Let mixture cool. Then add celery, apples and nuts. Pour in pan. Chill 24 hours before serving.

PURPLE LADY SALAD

1 3-oz. box grape Jello
8 oz. crushed pineapple, drained
¼ tsp. blueberry flavoring
2 C. miniature marshmallows

1 C. boiling water
1 can blueberry pie filling
2 C. prepared whipped topping

Dissolve Jello in water. Let set until syrupy. Add pineapple, pie filling and flavoring. Fold in topping and marshmallows. Pour into dish and let set until firm. This is best if made and set overnight.

ORANGE VEGETABLE SALAD

1 box orange Jello
1 C. boiling water
1 C. Miracle Whip
1 C. small curd cottage cheese, undrained

1 C. grated carrots
1 small onion, diced
1 C. diced celery
⅓ C. diced green pepper

Mix Jello and boiling water. While hot, add Miracle Whip, and cool. Then add rest of ingredients and stir and chill.

HERB'S FAVORITE OIL DRESSING

½ C. sugar
½ C. vinegar
½ C. oil

1 tsp. garlic salt
Salt, to taste
Pepper, to taste

Put ingredients in jar and shake and shake.

APRICOT TAPIOCA SALAD

2 pkg. vanilla tapioca pudding
1 can apricots (cut up)
1 tub Cool Whip

1 can crushed pineapple
1 3-oz. box orange Jello

Drain pineapple and apricots. Combine fruit juice with enough water to make three cups. Bring to boil. Add tapioca and return to rolling boil. Remove from heat. Add Jello, stir and cool. Add fruit and Cool Whip. Makes a large salad.

BLUE CHEESE DRESSING

1 pkg. cream cheese
¼ to ½ C. blue cheese salad dressing
2 or 3 green onions (chopped, use part of top)

Sour cream, if handy
¾ pt. mayonnaise

Mix all together. Add milk to thin if you need to later.

ELSIE'S SALAD

¼ C. sugar
¼ C. vinegar
2 T. butter
2 large eggs, beaten

1 carton Cool Whip
2 C. small marshmallows
1 can fruit cocktail (drained)

Cook sugar, vinegar, butter and eggs until thick and cool in refrigerator. Mix together with Cool Whip, marshmallows and fruit cocktail.

STRAWBERRY SALAD

3 pkg. strawberry Jello
2 boxes frozen strawberries
1 large box (8 oz.) Cool Whip

3¾ C. hot water
1 3-oz. pkg. cream cheese
½ C. chopped pecans

Dissolve 2 pkg. Jello in 2½ C. hot water. Add strawberries, including juice. Let set in 9 x 12-inch container until firm. Dissolve 1 pkg. Jello in 1¼ C. hot water. When partially jelled, beat into softened cream cheese. Add Cool Whip and nuts. Spread on first layer and chill.

Variations: For bottom layer, dissolve 2 pkg. Jello in 3½ C. hot water. When cool, add 3 or 4 bananas, sliced. Let set and add top layer.

Peach: Dissolve 2 pkg. peach Jello in 3½ C. hot water. Add 1#2½ can sliced peaches and ½ tsp. almond extract. Use peach Jello for top layer. Serves 12-15.

MAIN DISHES

7 SEAS CASSEROLE

1 can celery soup
½ tsp. salt
¼ C. onions (chopped fine)
1½ C. peas (I like frozen)
1 can light flaked tuna (drained)

1½ C. water
Dash of pepper
1⅓ C. minute rice
¾ C. grated Cheddar cheese

In a saucepan put soup, water, salt, pepper and onions. Bring to a boil. Layer the other ingredients in a flat bake dish and pour the soup mixture over. Save enough cheese for top of casserole. Bake 25 minutes at 375°.

WILD RICE CASSEROLE

1 pkg. wild & long grain rice
½ C. margarine
1 stalk celery
1 onion

1 can mushroom soup
1 can mushrooms & juice
½ lb. Velveeta cheese

I use Uncle Ben's 6 oz. pkg. rice. Cook as directed but do not use the package of herbs. Melt margarine. Add celery and onion. Add mushroom soup and mushrooms with their juice. Add cheese and heat until melted. Put all in a casserole and let stand 1 hour or overnight. Bake at 350° for 1 hour.

53

CHICKEN CASSEROLE

3 C. diced chicken
1 can mushroom soup
½ C. chicken broth

¼ C. chopped onion
1 C. diced celery
2 C. chow mein noodles

Mix together all ingredients except 1 C. of the noodles. Pour mixture into greased casserole. Sprinkle 1 C. of noodles on top and bake at 350° for 30 minutes or more. 1 C. of broken cashew nuts can be added if desired.

TUNA AND NOODLE DISH

1 pkg. noodles (cooked)
1 can cream of chicken soup

1 can of cheese soup
1 can drained chunk tuna

Mix together and bake for 45 minutes at 350°.

RICE AND MEAT CASSEROLE

1 C. raw rice
2 lb. hamburger, uncooked
1 medium onion, chopped
1 green pepper, diced
1 C. grated carrot
½ lb. Velveeta cheese, cubed

1 tsp. salt
½ tsp. garlic salt
Pepper
4 C. milk
1 can cream of chicken soup
½ C. milk

Combine all ingredients (except soup and ½ C. milk) and let stand overnight or several hours. Bake covered at 325° for 2 hours. Combine soup and milk and spread on top of casserole. Bake uncovered 20 to 30 minutes more.

CHICKEN BROCCOLI CASSEROLE

2 10-oz. pkg. chopped broccoli
4 oz. can mushrooms (drained)
2 C. thick, white sauce
1½ C. Cheddar cheese
3 C. cooked chicken, chopped

½ tsp. poultry seasoning
1 medium onion, chopped
1 small can water chestnuts
2 oz. slivered almonds

Cook and drain broccoli. Saute mushrooms and onion in small amount of shortening. Make white sauce and add cheese. Cook on low heat till well blended. Combine all ingredients and pour into a 2½ quart casserole. May save some almonds for garnish on top of casserole. Bake at 375° for 25 to 30 minutes. May add shredded cheese the last few minutes of baking for garnish.

SAUSAGE WITH SWEET POTATO AND APPLE

½ lb. link sausage (cut in ½'' pieces)
2 medium-sized sweet potatoes
3 medium-sized apples
1 tsp. salt

1 T. flour
2 T. sugar
½ C. cold water
1 T. sausage drippings

Fry sausage until well done. Pare and slice potatoes and apples. Mix salt, flour, sugar and blend with cold water. Arrange layers of potatoes, sausages and apples in baking dish. Pour some of flour, sugar and water mixture over each layer. Top with apples and sausage. Add drippings. Cover and bake at 375° for about 45 minutes.

PARTY PIZZAS

6 English muffins (split in half)
2 to 3 T. butter, melted
1 lb. lean ground pork
Oregano

2 C. diced cheese, American or
   mozzarella
1 C. pizza sauce

Spread melted butter on muffin halves. Brown pork; drain. Add cheese (reserve a small amount for topping), pizza sauce, and oregano to taste. Spread on muffin halves. Broil or microwave till cheese begins to melt. Sprinkle remaining cheese over sandwiches and heat again till cheese melts.

MEAT AND BEAN CASSEROLE

1½ lb. hamburger
1 chopped onion
⅓ lb. chopped bacon
1 C. brown sugar
½ C. catsup
¼ C. mustard

1 can pork & beans
1 can green beans (drained)
1 can wax beans (drained)
1 can kidney beans (drained)
1 can butter beans (drained)

Brown hamburger, onion and bacon. Drain off grease and add brown sugar, catsup and mustard. Stir, then add rest of ingredients. Bake 1 hour at 350°.

GROUND BEEF VEGETABLE CASSEROLE

1 lb. ground beef
1 small onion, chopped
4 or 5 medium potatoes

1 can vegetable soup
1 can golden mushroom soup

Brown meat and onion. Peel and slice potatoes and add to meat. Blend in the soups, undiluted. Mix well and pour into a greased large casserole. Bake at 375° for at least 1 hour.

56

BRAISED LIVER CASSEROLE

1 lb. beef or lamb liver
¼ C. flour
1½ tsp. salt
¼ tsp. pepper
2 T. oil
2 carrots, sliced

1 onion, sliced
1 red pepper, chopped
2 potatoes, sliced
1 C. beef stock
½ lb. tomatoes, chopped
1 bay leaf

Cut liver into two-inch squares. Roll in flour, which has been seasoned with salt and pepper. Brown in hot oil. Remove liver and brown carrots, onion, pepper and potatoes. Remove vegetables. Blend remaining flour left from dredging liver into oil. Stir in beef stock and tomatoes. Combine gravy with liver and vegetables. Add bay leaf and pour into casserole dish; cover. Bake in a 350° oven for 1 hour. Serves 4.

EASY DEEP DISH PIZZA

3 C. Bisquick baking mix
¾ C. water
1 lb. ground beef
½ C. chopped onion
½ tsp. salt
2 cloves garlic, crushed

1 can (15 oz.) tomato sauce
1 tsp. Italian seasoning
4½ oz. jar sliced mushrooms, drain
½ C. chopped green pepper
2 C. shredded mozzarella cheese
(about 8 oz.)

Heat oven to 425°. Lightly grease jelly roll pan, 15½ x 10½ x 1-inch or cookie sheet. Mix baking mix and water until soft dough forms. Gently smooth dough into ball on floured surface. Knead 20 times. Pat dough on bottom and up sides of pan with floured hands. Or roll into rectangle, 13 x 10-inch and place on cookie sheet; pinch edges of rectangle, forming ¾-inch rim. Cook and stir ground beef, onion, salt and garlic until beef is brown; drain. Mix tomato sauce and Italian seasoning; spread evenly over dough. Spoon beef mixture evenly over sauce. Top with mushrooms, green pepper and cheese. Bake until crust is golden brown, about 20 minutes. 8 Servings.

57

EGG ROLLS

2½ lb. ground beef (or ½ beef & ½ pork)
3 chopped onions (or less if desired)
1 grated carrot
2½ tsp. salt
1½ tsp. pepper
2 tsp. sugar
4 tsp. cornstarch
6 eggs
2 pkg. small bean threads
    (can use chow mein noodles but
    soak in hot water 1st to soften)
3 pkg. egg rolls

Unwrap egg rolls and drop 1 T. of meat mixture on each egg roll and wrap up. Cook in 1-inch of grease in electric skillet 30 minutes. (These can be wrapped individually in wax paper and frozen for use later, but they do have to be thawed before frying.)

BRUNCH CASSEROLE

8 slices bread
1 lb. sausage (browned & drained)
2 C. grated Cheddar cheese
4 eggs, beaten
3 C. milk
¾ tsp. dry mustard
½ tsp. salt
1 C. mushroom soup

Place bread, sausage and cheese in layers in pan. Mix together eggs, 2½ C. milk, mustard and salt. Pour over cheese. Combine remaining milk and soup. Pour over all. Refrigerate overnight. Bake 1½ hours at 300°. Excellent with bran muffins and fresh cantalope or fruit ice.

HAM LOAF

1 lb. beef, ground
1 lb. ground fresh pork
1 lb. ground cured ham
1½ C. milk
3 eggs
1½ C. cracker crumbs
Tomato juice

Mix, adding tomato juice until correct consistency. Bake at 350° until done.

PORK CHOPS AND RICE

1 6-oz. pkg. white & wild rice (long grain)
1 onion
1 green pepper
1 tomato

Pork chops
1 can consomme
¼ C. white dry wine
1 C. water

Brown pork chops and put in casserole (covered). Put a slice of onion, green pepper and tomato on top of each chop. Soak rice in ice water 3 minutes and drain. Take 1 C. water, 1 can consomme and ½ C. white dry wine. Bring to boil and pour over rice. Spoon rice over chops and put in casserole. Bake at 350° for 1 hour.

DILL GRAVY

4 T. butter
4 T. flour
2 T. fresh dill weed

1¾ C. water
Salt & pepper, to taste

Melt butter in large, heavy skillet over medium heat. Add dill and cook slowly for three minutes. Add flour and brown gently, cooking the flour with the butter so the gravy will have a nice brown coloring. Stir with a fork to keep the gravy smooth. Slowly add water, stirring constantly. Bring to boiling point. Simmer for five minutes. Add more liquid for a thinner gravy. Season with salt and pepper.

MEAT LOAF

2 lb. ground beef
4 eggs
1 can Pet milk

¾ C. crushed corn flakes (¾)
1 tsp. salt

Combine all ingredients and put into a greased loaf pan. Sprinkle a little sugar and cream over this. Bake 1 hour in 350° oven.

SWEDISH MEATBALLS

3 lb. hamburger
3 pkg. dry onion soup

3 cans cream of mushroom soup
¾ can milk

Make hamburger into bite size balls. Brown and cook in pan. Add mushroom soup and the can of milk to meatballs. Add dry soup mix and stir gently. Put in Dutch oven and simmer at 250° as long as desired, stir often.

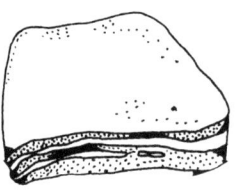

CHICKEN CASSEROLE

9 slices bread
4 C. diced, cooked chicken
1 can mushrooms (sauted in butter)
2 small cans water chestnuts (sliced & drained)
½ C. mayonnaise
9 slices sharp Cheddar cheese

4 eggs, well beaten
2 C. milk
1 tsp. salt
1 can mushroom soup
1 can celery soup
Few pimentos
Butter

Remove crusts from 9 slices of bread and place in bottom of a buttered pan. Top with 4 C. chicken, mushrooms and water chestnuts. Spread mayonnaise over this and top with slices of cheese. Beat eggs with milk; add salt and pour over mixture in pan; mix. Mix mushrooms and celery soup and pimentos and pour over top, cover with foil and refrigerate for 24 hours. Bake 1½ hours at 350°. Crumb crusts and brown with butter and put on top the last 15 minutes.

FAKE STEAK

3 lb. hamburger
1 C. bread crumbs
3 tsp. salt

Pepper to taste
Medium onion
1 C. milk

Mix and spread on cookie sheet. Chill overnight. Cut in squares, coat with flour and brown lightly. Put in a tightly covered pan. Pour 1 can cream of mushroom soup over and bake at 350° for 1 hour.

60

DESSERTS

OREO COOKIE DELIGHT

1 lb. pkg. Oreo cookies (crushed)
½ C. oleo (1 stick), melted
½ gallon vanilla ice cream (softened)
1 lb. salted peanuts (optional)
1 13-oz. can evaporated milk

½ C. oleo
⅔ C. chocolate chips
2 C. powdered sugar
1 tsp. vanilla (optional)

Crush cookies into crumbs; combine with melted oleo and press into lightly greased 9 x 13-inch pan. Soften ice cream and spread over cookie crust. If using the peanuts spread evenly over the ice cream. Combine chocolate chips, oleo, evaporated milk and powdered sugar. Cook 8 to 10 minutes over low heat. Cool and add vanilla if desired. Spread chocolate sauce over ice cream and store in freezer. To serve cut into squares. (Make chocolate sauce first so it can cool while you prepare the other two layers.)

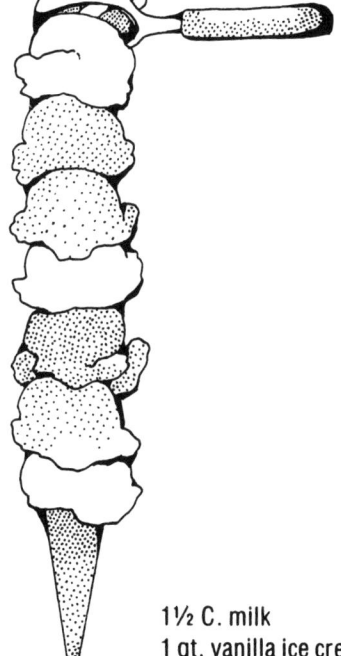

ICE CREAM DESSERT

65 Ritz crackers (crushed)
1 stick margarine (melted)
2 pkg. instant chocolate pudding

1½ C. milk
1 qt. vanilla ice cream (softened)
1 carton Cool Whip

Mix together crackers and margarine; reserve 1 C. of crumbs and pat remainder in a 9 x 13-inch pan. Beat together for 2 minutes the pudding and milk, then blend in softened ice cream. Pour over cracker crust and top with Cool Whip. Sprinkle with remaining crumbs and refrigerate. You may use any flavor of pudding or ice cream you desire. It is good with a graham cracker crust as well.

63

BREAD PUDDING

2 C. bread crumbs	4 C. milk
⅓ C. sugar	2 eggs
½ tsp. salt	1 tsp. vanilla
¼ tsp. cinnamon	

VARIATIONS:

1 C. raisins	2 sq. or 3 T. cocoa & ¼ C. sugar
¼ C. chopped nuts	Use fruit jam instead of sugar

Stir all ingredients together and put in a greased baking dish and bake 1 hour in a slow oven.

BANANA DELIGHT

1 pkg. graham crackers	1 box instant vanilla pudding
3 bananas	4 C. milk
1 box instant lemon pudding	

Crush graham crackers in a plastic bag. Reserve ¼ C. crumbs; place remaining crumbs in the bottom of a 6 x 10-inch Pyrex dish. Mix the milk with the puddings and stir until well blended. (A blender works well to mix up the pudding.) Spread a very thin coating of pudding over the crumbs! Slice the bananas ½-inch thick and place on the pudding. Pour the remaining pudding over the bananas, making sure the bananas are completely covered with the pudding. Sprinkle with reserved crumbs over the top and then refrigerate pudding until completely cooled and set.

ROMANCE

APPETIZERS

&

BEVERAGES

DILLY CHEDDAR BALL

1 8-oz. pkg. cream cheese
¼ lb. butter or margarine
¼ C. green onion, chopped
¼ C. dill pickle, chopped
2 oz. Cheddar cheese (grated)

1 T. Worcestershire sauce
¼ tsp. salt
Dash red pepper
Pecans

GLAZE:
1 C. honey
1 C. catsup

½ C. cider vinegar

Use ¼ C. of glaze on the cheese ball and serve remaining with cooked roast.

SALMON PARTY BALL

1 can red salmon, drained & flaked
1 T. lemon juice
1 tsp. prepared horseradish
¼ tsp. liquid smoke
1 8-oz. pkg. cream cheese, softened

2 tsp. grated onion
½ tsp. salt
½ C. chopped pecans
3 T. snipped parsley

Make cheese ball and chill several hours, then roll in the snipped parsley and pecans.

PUNCH

1 pkg. lemon Kool-Aid
1 pkg. lemon-lime Kool-Aid
1 lb. 14 oz. can pineapple juice

2 C. sugar
1 gallon water
1 large bottle 7-Up

Mix all except the 7-Up and add it just before serving.

69

SHRIMP OR CRAB DIP

1 can shrimp or crab meat
1 small onion, minced
1 8-oz. pkg. cream cheese
Sprinkle on onion salt

¼ tsp. horseradish
Pinch of garlic salt
Dash of Worcestershire sauce
Milk to soften cream cheese

Mix and bake in covered dish at 325° for ½ hour. Grate cheese over top and return to oven long enough for cheese to melt.

MEXICAN DIP

1 lb. Velveeta
1 lb. Cheddar cheese

2 tomatoes, chopped
1 jar jalapeno (small jar)

Bake for ½ hour at 250°. Can use corn chips on the bottom of dish or use as a dip.

CHILI CON QUESTO

1 small Velveeta cheese
1 16-oz. Hormel chili (without beans)

Small amount of milk

Melt cheese in milk in microwave or double boiler. Add chili and put in fondue pot. Serve with crackers or taco chips.

BANANA PUNCH (30-40 Cups)

7 large bananas, pureed
4 C. sugar
6 C. water
1 46-oz. can pineapple juice

2 12-oz. can frozen orange juice
1 12-oz. frozen lemon concentrate
2 8-oz. can lemon-lime soda

Heat sugar and water; cool. Add all the other and freeze. Just before serving (2 hours) remove from freezer and add the lemon-lime soda. Can be tinted any color.

CHEESE BALL

2 8-oz. pkgs. cream cheese   Chili sauce
Form cream cheese into a ball and pour chili sauce over.

PINA COLADA PUNCH

1 46-oz. can pineapple juice, chilled
1 16-oz. can creme of coconut

1 qt. vanilla ice cream
1 28-oz. bottle chilled club soda

Combine pineapple juice and coconut; mix. Spoon in ice cream. Slowly add soda. Serve immediately. Serves 12-14.

INSTANT COCOA MIX

1 8-qt. pkg. instant dry milk
1 9-oz. jar Coffee Mate
2 C. powdered sugar

1 lb. box Nestles Quick
1 pkg. instant vanilla pudding
Vanilla

Mix all in large container. To use, fill cup ⅓ to ½ full of powdered mix and add hot water. For large amounts, use 1⅓ C. to 1 quart of hot water.

PINEAPPLE RUBY PUNCH

1 pt. cranberry juice
1 46-oz. can pineapple juice

1 28-oz. bottle soda
½ C. lemon juice

Have all ingredients well chilled. Combine and serve. Makes 25 punch cup servings.

HOT CRANBERRY PUNCH

2½ C. pineapple juice
2 C. cranberry juice cocktail
1¾ C. water
½ C. brown sugar

3 sticks cinnamon
½ T. whole allspice
1 T. whole cloves
¼ tsp. salt

In percolator basket combine the dry ingredients. Perk for a few minutes. Serves 8-10.

CANDY

&

COOKIES

CHEWY BUTTERSCOTCH BARS

1 stick butter or oleo
1½-2 C. brown sugar
2 eggs
1½ C. flour

2 tsp. baking powder
1 tsp. vanilla
½ to 1 C. nuts or coconut

Melt butter in saucepan. Add sugar and bring to boil over low heat, stirring constantly. Cool slightly. Drop in eggs, 1 at a time and mix well. Add vanilla and dry ingredients. Stir in nuts or coconut. Press into greased 13 x 9-inch pan. Bake at 350° for 20-30 minutes.

CEREAL COOKIES

1 C. sugar
1 C. brown sugar
1 C. shortening
2 eggs plus 1 T. water
2 C. flour
½ tsp. salt

1 tsp. baking powder
1 C. shredded coconut
1 tsp. vanilla
1 C. oatmeal
1 C. Rice Krispies

Drop and bake in a moderate oven.

CHERRY BARS

1 C. oleo
1½ C. sugar
3 eggs
1 tsp. vanilla

1½ t. baking powder
2¼ C. flour
1 can cherry pie filling

Do not grease pan. Beat oleo, sugar and eggs together. Add vanilla, baking powder and flour. Put ⅔ of batter in baking pan. Spread pie filling on batter. Top with remaining batter. Bake at 350° for 25-30 minutes. Frost with powdered sugar frosting.

ICED BUTTERSCOTCH CHIPS

½ C. shortening   1½ C. brown sugar
2 eggs   1 C. thick sour cream
1 tsp. vanilla   2¾ C. flour
½ tsp. soda   ½ tsp. baking powder
½ tsp. salt   ⅔ C nuts or coconut (optional)

   Mix all ingredients and drop by spoonfuls on cookie sheet. Bake at 400° for 10 minutes. While warm spread with icing.

ICING:
4 T. oleo   ½ tsp. vanilla
1 C. powdered sugar   Hot water

   Heat oleo until brown. Blend in powdered sugar, vanilla and enough hot water to make spreadable.

CHOCOLATE CHIP COOKIES

⅔ C. shortening or margarine   1 tsp. salt
1 C. granulated sugar   2¼ C. flour
½ C. brown sugar   1 tsp. soda
2 tsp. vanilla   1 6-oz. pkg. chocolate chips
2 eggs

   Cream shortening and sugar. Beat in eggs. Mix dry ingredients and sift into mixture. Stir well. Add vanilla and chocolate chips. Dough should be fairly stiff. Place teaspoonfuls on lightly greased baking sheets, about 2'' apart. Bake 10 to 12 minutes at 350°. Bake 8 to 10 minutes for softer cookie. Makes 4 dozen.

BREADS

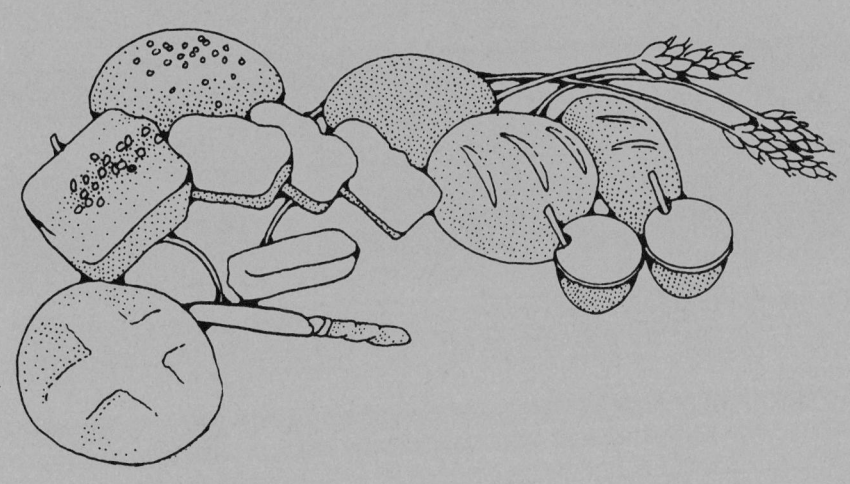

RAISED DOUGHNUTS

1½ C. scalded milk
2 eggs
¾ C. sugar
5 C. flour

2 pkg. yeast
1 tsp. salt
⅓ C. butter
1 C. mashed potatoes

GLAZE:
1 lb. powdered sugar
Butter, size of egg
1 tsp. vanilla

1 T. cornstarch
1 T. cream

Boil and mash potatoes, while still hot add butter, beaten eggs, sugar and milk. When mixture is lukewarm, add yeast. When it is dissolved, add salt and flour. Let rise. Punch down and let rise again. Roll to ½-inch in thickness. Cut with cookie cutter. Instead of cutting a hole in the center, pull a hole about the size of a 50 cent piece with fingers. Let rise, then fry in hot fat. Add enough water to make a thin frosting. Dip doughnuts in frosting then string on spoon handle to drip. When nearly dry stand on edge on waxed paper.

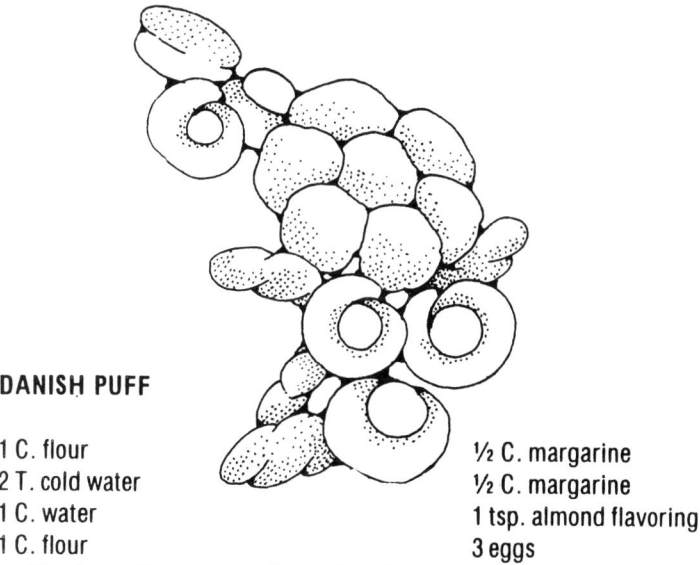

DANISH PUFF

1 C. flour
2 T. cold water
1 C. water
1 C. flour

½ C. margarine
½ C. margarine
1 tsp. almond flavoring
3 eggs

Mix flour, ½ cup margarine and cold water, like pie crust. Roll into ball. Divide into 2 parts. Pat onto cookie sheet into 3 x 12-inch strips. Bring margarine and water to rolling boil. Remove from heat and add almond flavoring. Stir in flour, all at once, until smooth and thick. Add eggs, 1 at a time, and spread mixture on top of crust. Bake 60 minutes in 350° oven. Top with powdered sugar frosting, slightly colored if desired.

EASY CINNAMON ROLLS

2 loaves frozen bread
1 C. brown sugar
½ tsp. cinnamon
½ tsp. vanilla

½ C. oleo
1 pkg. reg. butterscotch pudding
½ C. milk

Thaw bread in refrigerator overnight. Keep in plastic bag to keep from drying out. Melt oleo and add sugar, pudding, cinnamon, vanilla and milk. Slice dough and put in a 9 x 13-inch cake pan and stir up sugar mixture and pour over dough, then let rise. Bake in 350° oven for 30 minutes or until done. Turn upside down after taking out of oven so pudding mixture will be on top.

BLUEBERRY COFFEECAKE

1 C. blueberries
½ C. margarine
½ C. shortening
1 tsp. vanilla
1 tsp. baking powder
¼ tsp. salt
⅓ C. pecans

⅔ C. brown sugar
2 tsp. cinnamon
1 C. sugar
2 C. flour
1 tsp. soda
2 C. sour cream

Grease a bundt pan. Blend brown sugar, butter and cinnamon together; set aside. Cream shortening and granulated sugar. Add eggs, 1 at a time, until smooth and creamy; add vanilla. Add dry ingredients and sour cream in portions alternately. Pour half the batter into pan. Sprinkle half of reserved mixture and the blueberries. Cover with remaining batter. Mix remaining topping with pecans and sprinkle over top. Bake at 350° for 45-55 minutes.

HANDY ROLL MIX

1 C. milk
3 T. sugar
1 egg
¼ C. warm water

2 T. shortening
1 tsp. salt
1 cake yeast
3 C. flour

Bring milk, shortening, sugar and salt to a boil; then cool to lukewarm. Add egg and yeast dissolved in water. Mix in 3 C. flour. Makes a soft dough. Let rise until double in bulk, then roll out and fix to suit taste.

PUMPKIN BREAD

3 C. sugar
4 eggs
1½ tsp. salt
1 tsp. cinnamon
⅔ C. water

1 C. oil or shortening
3⅓ C. flour
2 tsp. soda
1 tsp. nutmeg
2 C. pumpkin

Combine sugar, oil and eggs; mix well. Combine dry ingredients and add to egg mixture. Add water and pumpkin and mix well. Bake in 3 bread pans or 5 small loaf pans. Test with a toothpick inserted in center of loaf. Bake at 350° for 1 hour.

RICH SHORTCAKE

2 C. flour
4 tsp. baking powder
Few grains of nutmeg
1 egg

¼ C. sugar
½ tsp. salt
½ C. margarine
⅓ C. milk

Mix dry ingredients. Work in margarine with pastry blender until it looks like cornmeal. Mix in beaten egg with spoon. Mix in milk gradually. Put dough in greased 8'' pan. Pat down with palm of hand. Bake 12 minutes at 450°.

81

ZUCCHINI BREAD

3 eggs
3 tsp. vanilla
3 C. flour
2 C. grated zucchini
1 tsp. baking soda
3 tsp. cinnamon
1 C. oil

1 tsp. salt
¼ C. chopped nuts
1½ C. sugar
¼ tsp. baking powder
¼-⅓ C. raisins, dates or
   cherries

Beat eggs well and add oil, sugar, zucchini and vanilla. Beat well. Combine dry ingredients and mix well; add nuts. Bake at 325° for 40 minutes to 1 hour.

ROLLS

2 pkg. dry yeast
2 C. flour
1 T. sugar
½ C. butter
2 eggs

½ C. warm water
2 C. scalded milk
5 C. flour
⅓ C. sugar
2 tsp. salt

Dissolve yeast, beat 2 cups flour and cooled milk. Add yeast, sprinkle with the sugar. Let stand until bubbly. Add the following creamed mixture: butter, ⅓ C. sugar, eggs and salt. Then add flour and knead until smooth and elastic. Bake at 350°.

VEGGIES

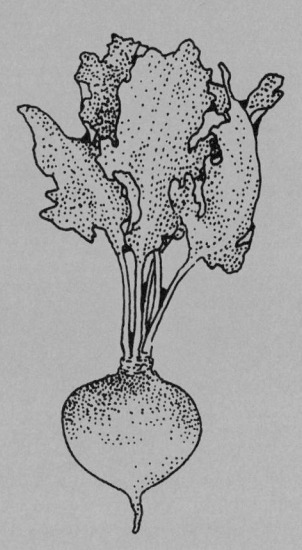

CUCUMBERS IN SOUR CREAM

1 large cucumber
½ C. sour cream
¼ tsp. dill seed

¾ tsp. salt
1 T. sugar
Pepper & vinegar

Pare and thinly slice cucumber. Put slices in shallow dish, sprinkle with salt. Add vinegar and let stand 30 minutes and drain. Combine remaining ingredients. Toss with cucumbers. Chill 1 hour.

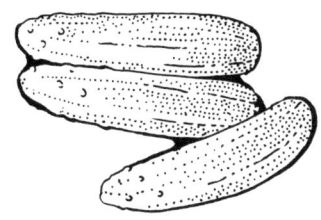

POTATO KUGELIS

10 large potatoes
1 medium onion
5 slices bacon
2 tsp. salt

¼ tsp. pepper
½ C. hot milk
3 eggs

Peel and grate fine the potatoes and onions. Cut the bacon crosswise into narrow strips, fry until crisp. Pour fat and bacon over potatoes. Add hot milk. Add eggs, 1 at a time and salt and pepper. Pour into greased pan. Bake at 400° for 15 minutes. Reduce heat to 375° for 15 minutes longer. Serve hot with sour cream.

POTATO CASSEROLE

1 2-lb. bag frozen hash browns
1 C. chopped onion
1 can cream of chicken soup
1 tsp. garlic salt
2 C. corn flake crumbs

1½ stick butter
8 oz. grated Cheddar cheese
1 tsp. salt
1 pt. sour cream (16 oz.)

Defrost potatoes. Mix ingredients. Reserve ½ stick of butter and corn flake crumbs. Pour into 9 x 13-inch pan. Top with buttered crumbs. Bake at 350° for 1½ hours.

85

ONION PATTIES

¾ C. flour
2 tsp. baking powder
1 T. sugar
½ tsp. salt
1 T. cornmeal

½ C. powdered milk
Cold water
2½ C. finely chopped onions
Fat, for frying

Mix everything except water, onions and fat. Stir in enough cold water for thick batter. Mix in onions and drop by teaspoonfuls into deep fat. Flatten patties slightly as you turn them. Fry to a golden brown.

THREE VEGETABLE CASSEROLE

1 (10 oz.) box frozen lima beans
1 (10 oz.) box frozen cauliflower
1 (10 oz.) box frozen broccoli
1 (10 oz.) can cream of
    mushroom soup

1 C. Velveeta cheese cubed or
    a small jar of Cheez Whiz
2 T. milk
1 can French fried onion rings
    (like Burke)

Cook lima beans, according to package directions. Pour boiling water over the cauliflower and broccoli and cook slightly. Drain liquid. Combine soup, cheese and milk in saucepan and heat until well blended. Pour over the vegetables that have been put together in a greased casserole dish. Bake 30 to 40 minutes at 350°. During the last 10 minutes, cover with the onion rings.

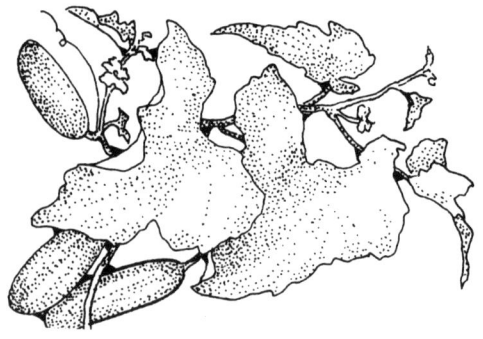

BROCCOLI WITH RICE (Serves 6)

1 stick butter
1 onion, chopped
1 rib of celery
1 pkg. frozen chopped broccoli
Tabasco
1½ C. cooked rice

Salt & pepper, to taste
Bread crumbs
Dash of Lawrys seasoned salt
1 C. grated cheese
1 can cream of chicken soup

In a large skillet, saute onions and celery until vegetables are clear. Cook broccoli, drain well. Mix broccoli with soup and cheese; add to celery and onions. Stir in rice, seasoning and mix well. Put into greased casserole and top with bread crumbs. Bake at 350° for 45 minutes. This can be made ahead and frozen.

CORN NOODLE CASSEROLE

8 oz. pkg. noodles
1 stick oleo

8 oz. Velveeta cheese
1 can cream style corn

Cook, cool and drain noodles. Add oleo, cheese and corn. Top with crumbs and bake in moderate oven until brown.

BROCCOLI CASSEROLE

2 pkg. frozen chopped broccoli
1 can mushroom soup
1 C. grated Cheddar cheese
1 stick oleo
½ C. milk

2 eggs
1 medium onion (chopped)
2 C. Pepperidge farm
   dressing bread

    Cook broccoli until done and drain. In saucepan, put mushroom soup, milk, and beaten eggs. Add dash of salt and pepper. Put on stove and heat at low temperature. When mixture is warm enough to melt cheese, add your grated cheese and chopped onion. Put in greased casserole dish, a layer of broccoli and sauce. Another layer of broccoli and then the rest of the sauce. In another pan, melt the oleo with the dressing mix. Sprinkle over the top and bake at 350° for 40 minutes.

GREEN BEAN HOT DISH

1 qt. green beans
¾ C. cooked hamburger
1 small chopped onion

1 chopped green pepper
1 can cream of mushroom soup
Grated cheese

    Cook green beans. Layer beans and hamburger, mixed onion and green pepper. Mix soup with ¼ can of water or milk and pour over top. Sprinkle grated cheese over top and heat in oven until it bubbles.

88

SOUPS

&

SANDWICHES

DIET VEGETABLE SOUP

3 stalks celery, chopped
½ head cabbage, chopped
2 cans French style green beans
½ green pepper
1 T. dry minced onion

12 oz. tomato juice
1 chicken boullion cube
2 beef boullion cubes
1-2 T. soy sauce

Boil all for 1 hour until vegetables are done.

BEEFBURGERS

1 pt. water
1 minced onion
¾ C. or more catsup
2 tsp. chili powder
1 T. vinegar
1 T. brown sugar

1 T. prepared mustard
1 T. Worcestershire sauce
2 tsp. salt
Pepper
2 lb. hamburger

Boil the first four ingredients 7 minutes. Then add remaining ingredients. Cook about 35 minutes. If necessary, it may be thickened with quick oatmeal, or it can be thinned with tomato juice to the right consistency.

LARGE QUANTITY OYSTER SOUP

2½ qt. oysters, with liquor
1 C. melted butter
¼ C. salt

¼ tsp. pepper
1 tsp. Worcestershire sauce
9 qt. milk

Heat oysters in oyster liquor and butter, until edges curl. Add salt, pepper and Worcestershire sauce. Heat milk to boiling temperature, but do not boil. Add milk to oysters for about 10 minutes, before serving.

TOMATO SOUP

½ bushel tomatoes
1 bunch celery
5 onions
4 green or red peppers
7 sprigs parsley

11 cloves
4 bay leaves
½ C. sugar
¼ C. salt

Slice tomatoes without peeling. Cut up celery, onions, peppers and parsley. Cook until tender, then strain. You can boil and can this for seasoned juice or add ⅓ lb. melted butter and 7 T. of flour to the juice and make cream of tomato soup. Boil and can. Makes 9 quart.

PIZZA BURGERS

1 lb. ground beef
1 chopped onion
1 8-oz. can pizza sauce
1 small can mushrooms (or pieces)

½ lb. American cheese (grated)
Salt & pepper
Hamburger buns

Saute ground beef and onion until brown. Add mushrooms, spices, and pizza sauce; cool. Add cheese and spread on buns; broil.

COLD HAMBURGER SAUSAGE

2 lb. hamburger
1 C. water
¼ tsp. onion powder
¼ tsp. garlic powder

1 T. liquid smoke
1 T. brown sugar
2 T. Morton's Tender Quick
  curing salt

Mix the above ingredients together well and shape into 2-inch rolls. Wrap rolls in aluminum foil with shiny side in. Refrigerate for 24 hours. Remove from refrigerator and punch holes through foil with fork. Place on rack in baking pan and bake for 1½ hours at 325°. Unwrap and let cool. Rewrap in new foil and refrigerate. Serve as baloney or make sandwiches.

SALADS

FLORIDA POTATO SALAD

6 potatoes
2 cartons sour cream
1½ C. grated Cheddar cheese

1 onion, chopped fine
¼ C. butter
Cheese

Boil potatoes with the skins on in water to which you've added 2 bay leaves. Peel potatoes and mash them. Add the sour cream and cheese. Saute the onion in the butter; add to potato mixture. Place in a buttered casserole. Sprinkle with cheese. Bake in 350° oven until cheese melts and potatoes are hot, about 35 minutes.

KRAUT SALAD

1 No. 2 can kraut (drained)
1 C. sugar (mix with kraut)
½ C. green pepper (chopped)
   Mix all together.

½ C. celery (chopped)
¼ C. onion (chopped)
1 jar pimento pepper

NO-COOK SALAD DRESSING

1½ C. soybean oil
½ C. vinegar
⅓ C. sugar
1 tsp. salt

1 tsp. pepper
1 T. Worcestershire sauce
1 can tomato soup

Mix well in an electric blender. Store in glass container with 3 cut-up garlic buds.

SUMMER MACARONI SALAD

8 oz. shell macaroni (cooked & drained)
1 cucumber (diced)
1 small onion (chopped)
2 medium tomatoes (½'' pieces)
1 green pepper (diced)
2 hard boiled eggs (chopped)
2 tsp. prepared mustard

½ tsp. salt
1 T. sugar
¾-1 C. mayonnaise
¼ C. French dressing
2 tsp. vinegar or
 ⅓ C. sweet pickle relish

Combine all ingredients, toss together and cool.

FRENCH DRESSING

1 can Campbells tomato soup
1½ C. oil
¼ C. vinegar
½ to ¾ C. sugar
1 T. prepared mustard

1 T. Worcestershire sauce
1 T. Heinz 57 Sauce
Salt, to taste
3 cloves garlic
Dash of hot sauce

Mix together.

SPAGHETTI SALAD

8 oz. spaghetti (1½'' pieces, cook & cool)
1 small onion (chopped)
1 chopped green pepper

⅔ C. cubed Longhorn cheese
1 pkg. Mozzarella cheese (grated)
Salt & pepper

DRESSING:
1 C. Miracle Whip
½ C. Italian creamy dressing

1½ tsp. Presti seasoning

Mix together and chill. Before serving, cut up fresh tomatoes and add to salad.

96

FRUIT SALAD DRESSING

1 orange
1 lemon
1 lime

1 egg
¾ C. sugar

Place over medium heat, the juice and grated rind of orange lemon and lime, the egg and sugar. Stirring constantly bring to a boil for 1 minute. Can be refrigerated. Great on vanilla ice cream.

JOSEPH'S COAT SALAD

⅓ C. cider vinegar
½ C. water
2 T. cornstarch
¾ C. sugar
2 T. prepared mustard

2 pkg. (10 oz.) frozen veg. or 2 cans
    mixed veg. (cooked & drained)
½ C. diced celery
½ C. chopped onion
1 small jar chopped pimento

Mix vinegar, water, cornstarch, sugar and mustard and cook until thick. While hot pour over the vegetable mixture.

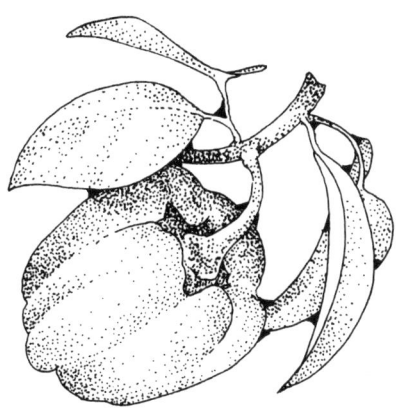

MARINATED VEGETABLES

1 lb. carrots (sliced)
1 small head Cauliflower (separated)
1 medium onion (sliced)
1 green pepper (chopped)
1 can tomato soup

1 tsp. mustard
1 C. sugar
1 C. salad oil
¾ C. vinegar
1 tsp. Worcestershire sauce

Cook carrots and cauliflower in water until barely tender. Drain and cool. Add onion and green pepper. Make dressing of the remaining ingredients and pour over vegetables. Marinate in refrigerator for at least 24 hours. Stir briskly before serving.

KRAUT SALAD

1 No. 2½ can kraut
2 C. celery, cut fine
1 tsp. celery seed
2 medium onions, chopped
    Keeps well in refrigerator.

1 or 2 green peppers, chopped
⅔ C. sugar
2 T. oil

PINEAPPLE SALAD

1 can crushed pineapple (drain & save juice)
1 lb. small marshmallows
1 egg

1 T. flour or cornstarch
1 C. sour cream

    Drain juice from pineapple and thicken with egg and flour or cornstarch. Cook and cool. Stir in sour cream. Pour over the marshmallow and pineapple.

BROCCOLI AND CAULIFLOWER SALAD

1 head cauliflower
4 stalks broccoli

Medium onion, sliced
Green pepper, sliced in rings

DRESSING:
1 C. mayonnaise
¼ C. Country style dressing
½ C. sour cream
1 T. vinegar

Dash of Worcestershire sauce
Dash salt
Dash Tabasco sauce

    Separate cauliflower into flowerets, cut up broccoli. Hamburger onions are nice as they add color. Combine dressing and vegetables and refrigerate several hours or overnight.

PERFECTION SALAD

1 pkg. lemon Jello
1 C. hot water
½ C. sugar
¼ tsp. salt
½ C. Miracle Whip
½ C. cold water
2 tsp. vinegar

1½ C. shredded cabbage
1 C. chopped celery
1 carrot, chopped fine
1 green pepper, chopped fine
2 T. grated onion
½ C. sliced stuffed olives

   Dissolve Jello in boiling water. Mix sugar, salt and salad dressing with Jello. Let cool before adding vegetables.

CABBAGE SALAD

4 C. sugar
1 C. water
1 large bunch celery, diced
1 T. celery seed

2 C. vinegar
2 medium sized heads of cabbage
3 chopped peppers
1 T. mustard seed

   Bring sugar, vinegar and water to a good boil and let cool. Shred cabbage. Add 2 T. salt, stir, let stand at least 1 hour. Drain, press or squeeze out all water. Add diced celery, peppers, celery seed and mustard seed. Will keep a long period of time stored in refrigerator.

ORANGE DATE SALAD

1½ lb. dates
1 dozen oranges
1 dozen apples
2 C. nuts

1 pkg. coconut
2 pkg. Dream Whip, prepared
1 pkg. marshmallows

   Mix and chill. Serves 40.

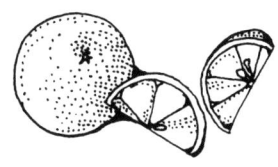

OUT OF THIS WORLD SALAD

1 can cherry pie filling
12 oz. can crushed pineapple
1 T. cornstarch
¾ C. sugar
1 tsp. red food coloring
1 3-oz. pkg. raspberry Jello
6 bananas
1 C. chopped pecans

Mix cherry pie filling, pineapple, cornstarch, sugar and red food coloring and cook until thick. Add Jello, and cool. Add bananas and pecans. Pour into large dish and chill until set.

SHRIMP SALAD

1 6-oz. pkg. frozen shrimp
5 hard boiled eggs, chopped
1 C. macaroni shells
½ C. diced Velveeta cheese
1 C. diced or chopped celery
½ C. minced onion or
    dash of onion salt
4 drops Tabasco sauce
1 T. garlic salt
6 T. mayonnaise

Cook shrimp. Cook macaroni and drain. Combine all ingredients and put in the refrigerator. Chill before eating.

TACO SALAD

1 head lettuce
1 can kidney beans (drained)
2-4 chopped tomatoes
1 onion, chopped
1 lb. ground beef
1 pkg. taco seasoning
1 bag taco corn chips
8 oz. Cheddar cheese, shredded
Hot taco sauce

Clean and tear lettuce. Cook ground beef and add taco seasoning, following directions. Mx all ingredients together. Add Cheddar cheese to top. Serve with hot sauce.

DELIGHTFUL EASTER SALAD

1 C. rice (cooked & cooled)
1 15-oz. can chunk pineapple (drained)
1 C. red grapes (halved & seeded)
1 C. green grapes

1 beaten egg
2 T. flour
1 tsp. lemon juice

Add pineapple and grapes to rice. In saucepan over low heat, cook the juice from pineapple, adding water to make 1 C., egg flour and lemon juice until thick and smooth. Cool and whip 1 C. cream, adding 1 tsp. vanilla and 1 tsp. sugar. Add the cooled pineapple sauce and whipped cream mixture to the rice and fruit. Fold in 5 oz. colored miniature marshmallows. Chill overnight. At serving time add 4 diced bananas.

SPRING SALAD

3 large yellow apples, diced
1 can crushed pineapple, drained
1 C. cooked applesauce
½ C. sugar
1 pkg. orange Jello

½ C. small marshmallows
Cool Whip
Red hots, crushed
1 C. crushed walnuts

Mix apples, crushed pineapple, applesauce and sugar. Then dissolve Jello in hot water and let cool. Then add all to Jello. Let stand until set. Then add marshmallows and top with Cool Whip. Then top with crushed red hots, then the walnuts. Let stand 2 or 3 hours to serve. 6-8 servings.

ANGEL HASH SALAD

2 T. cornstarch
¼ C. sugar
1 C. pineapple syrup & water
1 C. heavy cream (whipped)

2½ C. crushed pineapple (drained)
¼ C. chopped nuts
15 marshmallows (quartered)
6 bananas (sliced)

Combine cornstarch and sugar; add pineapple syrup gradually, stirring to blend well. Cook, stirring constantly until thickened. Add part of mixture to beaten egg yolks (2). Blend well and return to hot mixture. Cook stirring constantly for 2 minutes. Cool fold in whipped cream, pineapple, nuts and marshmallows. Chill overnight. Add sliced bananas, shortly before serving. Garnish with cherries and serve in lettuce lined bowl.

CRANBERRY SALAD

2 C. cranberries
2 C. water
1 C. sugar
2 pkg. cherry Jello
½ C. nuts

1 C. pineapple juice
1 C. drained crushed pineapple
1 C. unpeeled ground apple
1 C. ground celery

TOPPING:
1 3-oz. pkg. cream cheese
1 C. sour cream

⅓ C. sugar
1 T. lemon juice

Cook cranberries in 2 C. water until soft. Add 1 C. sugar and boil again. Remove from heat and add 2 pkg. cherry Jello. Dissolve and add 1 C. pineapple juice. Allow to cool and partially set. Add celery, nuts, apples and pineapple. Pour into flat pan and chill. Cream the topping ingredients together. Put on top of Jello.

MAIN DISHES

TUNA SPAGHETTI BAKE

1 can tuna (2 is better)
½ pkg. spaghetti
1 can cream of mushroom soup
Slivered almonds

Pimento (entire jar)
1 can mushrooms
1 C. mozzarella cheese
Potato chips

Mix all ingredients together except potato chips. Put in baking dish and top with potato chips. Bake at 350° until brown.

CREOLE SHRIMP

2 medium onions (sliced
4 pieces celery (chopped)
2 T. fat or vegetable oil
1 tsp. salt
1 C. water
2 C. tomatoes
1 T. vinegar

1 tsp. sugar
1½ C. shrimp (med. or small)
2 T. chili powder
1 small can mushrooms
3 C. hot boiled rice
3 T. flour

Cook onions and celery until brown in fat. Add flour and salt and slowly add the water. Cook fifteen minutes. Add tomatoes, vinegar, sugar and chili powder. Add shrimp and mushrooms last and cook ten minutes longer. Serve on rice.

105

SCALLOPED TURKEY

1⅔ C. broth
1 C. milk
1 can cream of mushroom soup
1 can cream of chicken soup
1 C. diced Velveeta cheese
½ tsp. salt

1 small pimento
1 small onion (diced)
2 C. cut-up turkey
2 C. uncooked macaroni
½ pkg. frozen peas (optional)

Mix all together and put in greased 9 x 13-inch pan and refrigerate overnight. Bake next day for 1 hour at 350°. Let set for a while before serving.

MACARONI-SAUSAGE BAKE

1 lb. bulk pork sausage
½ C. chopped onion
3 oz. macaroni (or big C.)
1 can cream of mushroom soup or
   cream of celery soup

⅔ C. milk
3 eggs. slightly beaten
2 C. shredded cheese
   (American or Cheddar)

Cook sausage and onion until lightly browned. Place in casserole dish. Cook macaroni in salt water and drain. Put on top of meat. Combine soup and milk; heat. Slowly stir in eggs; add cheese. Pour over macaroni. Bake at 350° for 40 to 45 minutes.

SUPER CHICKEN CASSEROLE

1 family pack chicken
1 C. chopped celery
2 T. minced onion
1½ cans cream of chicken soup
1 C. salad dressing or mayonnaise
2 T. lemon juice

¾ tsp. salt
¼ tsp. pepper
1½ to 2 C. stuffing mix
3 T. butter, melted
1 C. slivered almonds

Stew chicken, remove meat from bones and cut in bite size pieces. Combine chicken with celery, onion, soup, salad dressing, lemon juice, salt and pepper. Spread in baking dish. Toss the stuffing mix with the melted butter and scatter over top of chicken layer. Sprinkle almonds on top. Bake at 350° for 30 to 40 minutes.

CHICKEN A LA KING CASSEROLE

¾ C. raw rice or 1½ C minute rice
1 can cream of mushroom soup
1 can cream of chicken soup

1 chicken, cut-up (may be skinned)
½-1 pkg. dry onion soup

Put rice and soups in bottom of cake pan. Layer pieces of chicken on top. Cover with foil. Bake 2 hours at 350°.

STUFFED CABBAGE

1 head cabbage
1 lb. ground beef
1 C. rice
1 egg

1 tsp. salt
¼ tsp. pepper
2 C. tomato juice
1 C. cabbage juice

Boil cabbage in salted water about 10 minutes. Mix ground beef, rice, egg, salt and pepper. Roll meat mixture into a ball and roll in cabbage leaf. Secure with toothpick. Line bottom of pot with extra cabbage leaves. Pour in tomato juice plus water left from boiling cabbage. Cook about 1½ hours.

SOUTHERN GUMBO

2 T. flour
2 T. butter
1 qt. Okra
1 large onion

1 each #2 can corn, tomatoes
3 or 4 C. water
1 medium size chicken (fried)
Rice

Brown flour in the butter. Cut Okra and onion and brown in this. Add #2 can corn and tomatoes. Add water and simmer 1 hour. Fry chicken until nicely browned and add to boiling mixture and cook until tender. Cook rice and add a spoonful as you serve the gumbo in soup plates.

HOBO DINNER

1 large hamburger patty
Sliced potatoes
Sliced carrots
Sliced cabbage

Salt
Pepper
1 T. dried onions or
   1 slice fresh onion

Put in foil in order given. Close foil tightly. Bake in 375° for 45 minutes.

TACOS

1 lb. hamburger
2 T. minced onion
¼ tsp. minced garlic
½ tsp. salt
2 T. chili powder
½ tsp. oregano
¼ tsp. cumin seed
2 T. sweet pepper flakes
1 can tomato sauce

Brown meat and onions. Add other ingredients and simmer for 1 hour. Serve in taco shells topping with lettuce, chopped tomatoes, chopped onion and shredded cheese.

IMPOSSIBLE LASAGNE PIE

½ C. creamed cottage cheese
¼ C. Parmesan cheese
1 lb. ground beef
1 tsp. oregano leaves
½ tsp. basil leaves
1 can (6 oz.) tomato paste
1 C. shredded mozzarella cheese
1 C. milk
⅔ C. Bisquick baking mix
2 eggs
1 tsp. salt
¼ tsp. pepper

Cook and drain ground beef. Heat oven to 400°. Grease pie plate 10 x 1½ inches. Layer cottage and Parmesan cheese in plate. Mix beef, herbs, paste and ½ C. mozzarella, spoon on top. Beat milk, baking mix, eggs, salt and pepper for 1 minute. Pour into plate and bake 30 to 35 minutes. Sprinkle with remaining mozzarella.

OVEN FRIED CHICKEN

1 fryer, cut up
1 stick oleo, melted
Salt

Pepper
Paprika
3-4 C. crushed Rice Krispies

Sprinkle salt, pepper, paprika into melted oleo. Dip pieces of chicken into oleo, then roll into Rice Krispies. Lay on cookie sheet. Bake 1 hour at 350°. This doesn't need to be turned.

HAMBURGER CASSEROLE

1 lb. hamburger
½ C. chopped onion
1/8 tsp. garlic
1/8 tsp. thyme
1/8 tsp. oregano
1 C. minute rice

1 can mushroom soup
6 stuffed olives (sliced)
1½ tsp. salt
1 lb. can tomatoes
3 slices cheese or more
2 bay leaves

Brown hamburger and drain. Add all ingredients, except cheese and bay leaves. Bring mixture to a boil. Simmer 5 minutes. Put in casserole dish. Top with cheese and bay leaves. Bake 30 minutes at 325°-350°.

CORNED BEEF CASSEROLE

6 or 8-oz. pkg. elbow macaroni
1 can cream of chicken soup
1 can cream of mushroom soup
½ lb. Velveeta cheese

½ C. chopped onion
1 C. milk
1 can corned beef

Cook and drain macaroni. Set aside to use last. Cook the soups, cheese, onion and milk till cheese is almost melted. Fold in cooked macaroni and corned beef (cut in chunks). Pour into large casserole and bake 45 minutes in 350° oven. This is good and serves 12 people.

SWISS SHIRRED EGGS

3 T. flour
2 T. butter
1½ C. milk
Seasoning

Eggs
Buttered bread crumbs or
    cracker crumbs
Grated cheese

Make a cream sauce using flour, butter, milk and seasoning. Put a spoonful of sauce in the bottom of greased egg dish, cover with 2 eggs and then cover eggs with buttered bread crumbs or cracker crumbs. Bake in moderate oven until whites have set. Sprinkle with grated cheese and return to oven until cheese melts.

BREAD AND EGG CASSEROLE

8 eggs
4 C. milk

1 lb. cheese
Bread crumbs

Put bread crumbs in the bottom of a 9 x 12-inch pan. Beat eggs and milk and put on top of first mixture. Then grate the cheese; put it on top of the above mixture. Cook for 45 minutes in 450° oven.

IOWA HAM ROLL

1 lb. ground ham
1½ lb. ground pork
2 C. soft bread crumbs
2 eggs, well beaten
1 C. milk
1 C. brown sugar, packed

1 tsp. dry mustard
½ C. water
½ C. horseradish sauce (opt.)
½ C. heavy cream, whipped or use
    ½ & ½ sour cream with
    ½ C. mayonnaise

Combine the first five ingredients. Form into balls larger than a golf ball. Place in 13 x 9 x 2-inch pan. Combine sugar, mustard, vinegar, water and whipped cream and beat until dissolved. May be served with horseradish sauce.

MEATBALLS

¾ C. oatmeal
1 C. milk
1 small onion

1 lb. ground beef
Salt & pepper

SAUCE:
2 T. sugar
2 T. 57 sauce
1 C. catsup

½ C. water
3 T. vinegar
½ onion

Make oatmeal, milk, onion, salt, pepper and ground beef into balls and brown. Cook sauce ten minutes and pour over meatballs and bake at 350° for 45 minutes.

GLAZED HAM BALLS

¾ lb. ground ham
¾ lb. ground pork
1½ C. dry bread crumbs
¾ C. milk
2 eggs, well beaten

1 C. brown sugar
¼ C. fruit juice
¼ C. vinegar
1 tsp. prepared mustard

Combine meat, bread crumbs, milk and eggs; mix well. Form into 8 or 9 balls and place in 8 x 8 x 2-inch baking pan. Mix brown sugar, juice, vinegar and mustard in a small saucepan and bring to a boil over medium heat. Boil 5 or 6 minutes. Pour over meatballs. Bake at 350° for 1 hour. Dip sauce over balls for serving. Pineapple, peach or orange juice may be used with this recipe.

DESSERTS

SALLY'S ORANGE DESSERT

2 box orange tapioca pudding
3 C. water (use pineapple juice
 for part of water)
1 can mandarin oranges (drained)
2 C. miniature marshmallows

1 box orange Jello
2 pkg. Dream Whip or Cool Whip
1 can (#211) crushed pineapple
 (drained)

Mix the orange tapioca pudding, orange Jello and 3 C. of water and cook slowly until clear, stirring constantly. Cool completely. Fix the Dream Whip according to directions and stir into the cooled mixture. Add the fruits and marshmallows and stir well; refrigerate.

GREEN MINT DESSERT

CRUST:
½ lb. graham crackers (crushed)
¼ C. white sugar

¾ C. margarine

Crush crackers; combine crumbs, sugar and margarine. Pat into baking dish. Bake 10 minutes at 350°; cool.

FILLING:
½ C. margarine
2 C. powdered sugar
3 egg yolks
2 (1 oz.) sq. unsweetened
 chocolate (melted)

3 egg whites (stiffly beaten)
½ gallon vanilla ice cream
1 tsp. mint flavoring
Green food coloring
Graham cracker crumbs

Cream margarine and powdered sugar together. Add egg yolks, 1 at a time and beat well. Add melted chocolate and blend together. Fold in stiffly beaten egg whites; spread over crust. Soften ice cream in refrigerator, then beat with mixer, blend in mint flavoring and green food coloring. Spread ice cream mixture over chocolate mixture. Sprinkle top with graham cracker crumbs and freeze.

DATE ROLL

1 lb. box graham crackers (crushed)
1 lb. seeded dates (chopped)
½ lb. marshmallows (cut small)

1 C. nuts (chopped)
1 C. whipping cream

Crush crackers and reserve 1 C. of crumbs. Add marshmallows and mix; add dates and nuts. Moisten with enough cream until mixture holds shape, being careful not to get it too moist. Roll in reserve cracker crumbs and chill in the refrigerator in waxed paper. Slice and serve with whipped cream.

DATE PUDDING

1 C. chopped dates
1 tsp. soda
1 C. boiling water
½ C. shortening
1 C. sugar

1½ C. flour
1 egg
1 tsp. vanilla
1 tsp. baking powder
½ C. chopped nuts

Pour boiling water over dates and soda and let stand until cool. Cream shortening and sugar; add date mixture and remaining ingredients. Pour into a greased 8 x 12-inch baking dish. Bake at 325° for 45 minutes. Spread on the topping while pudding is still warm.

TOPPING:
1 C. sugar
⅔ C. dates
½ C. boiling water

1 tsp. vanilla
½ C. chopped nuts

Cook together sugar, dates and water until thick. Remove from heat and add vanilla and nuts. Serve with whipped cream or ice cream.

POWER

APPETIZERS

&

BEVERAGES

PUNCH

1 large can pineapple juice	2 qt. gingerale
1 large can frozen orange juice	Red food coloring
½ gallon raspberry sherbet	

Mix first three ingredients. Add gingerale just before serving.

GUACAMOLE (4 Cups)

4 ripe avocados	2 green onions, chopped
2 T. fresh lemon juice	Salt & pepper, to taste
1 tomato, peeled & chopped fine	Garlic powder, to taste
1 whole mild green chile, chopped	

Peel, seed and mash avocados. Add lemon juice, tomato, green chile, onion, salt, pepper and garlic powder. The dip may be served at this point, and will be chunky or it may be processed in the blender if a smoother texture is desired. To prevent the guacamole from turning dark, place the avocado seeds on top of the dip and cover tightly with plastic wrap and refrigerate until serving time. This should not be made more than four hours before serving. Serve as a dip for fried tortilla chips. Endive leaves may also be used to scoop the dip.

HOLIDAY PUNCH

1 can frozen lemonade	1 qt. gingerale
1 can very berry Hawaiian punch	1 qt. 7-Up

Mix well, then add 1 gallon raspberry sherbet.

CHEESE BALL

1 lb. grated Cheddar cheese
1 lb. pkg. cream cheese
1 tsp. garlic powder
1½ tsp. chili powder

1½ tsp. paprika
½ C. mayonnaise
1 C. chopped pecans

Mix all ingredients. Shape into 2 balls. Roll in chopped pecans. Refrigerate. May be frozen.

PUNCH

3 pkg. lemon Kool-Aid
3 pkg. strawberry Kool-Aid
3 cans frozen orange juice

4 or 5 C. sugar
6 qt. water
7-Up

Mix all together and just before serving add 2 small bottles 7-Up or 1 large bottle.

CHEESE SPREAD

½ lb. American cheese
½ lb. Velveeta cheese
½ lb. Colby cheese
Grate cheeses altogether
1 4-oz. jar chopped pimento

1 dash Accent
1 T. sugar
1 pt. mayonnaise
1 T. mustard

Mix rest of ingredients together with cheese. Add garlic salt and onion if desired.

122

CHEESE STUFFED PEPPERS

4 small green peppers
1 8-oz. pkg. cream cheese, softened
2 T. milk
2 4-oz. pkgs. (2 C.) Cheddar cheese, shredded

¼ C. sweet pickle relish, drained
1 T. Worcestershire sauce
½ tsp. salt
1 C. chopped radishes

The day before serving, mix at medium speed the cream cheese and milk until smooth. Lower speed and beat in next four ingredients until well blended. Stir in radishes with spoon. Press mix firmly into pepper halves. Cover and refrigerate. Just before serving, cut each half pepper into 3rds. Serve with cold cuts and greens.

BEEF PUFF APPETIZERS

½ C. butter
1 C. flour

4 eggs
1 env. dry onion soup mix

FILLING:
2 C. ground cooked beef
¼ C. chopped pickles
Dash of catsup

Dash or Worcestershire sauce
3 T. mayonnaise

For puffs - preheat oven to 400°. Combine 1 C. water with butter and heat to boiling. Stir in flour all at once and stir constantly until mixture leaves sides of pan and forms a ball. Remove from heat. Shake soup mix through a sieve over flover mix to remove large pieces of onion. Beat in eggs, 1 at a time. Continue beating until mixture is smooth and velvety. For each bite size puff, put ½ tsp. of dough on ungreased baking sheet. Bake 12-15 minutes, or until dry. Cool. Cut puffs open and spoon in meat filling. (Packaged cream puff mix may be used instead.) For Filling: Mix all ingredients together and fill cream puffs.

CHEESE BALL

2 large cream cheese (softened)
1 pkg. shredded sharp Cheddar
1 tsp. minced onion, or dry soup
1 T. lemon juice

Dash of pepper
1 tsp. Worcestershire sauce
¼ tsp. garlic

Mix all together and form into 1 large ball or two small ones. Can add chopped dried beef pieces before making into balls or make balls and roll in chopped pecans. Or can roll in chili powder.

CHEESE APPETIZER

1 can Pillsbury crescent rolls (4 roll size)   1 round Gouda cheese

Roll out dough and pinch into a square. Unwrap cheese (be sure to get the wax coating off) and place on top of dough. Wrap the cheese with the dough, making sure the cheese is completely covered and no holes have poked through the dough. Baste with one beaten egg. Bake for 17 minutes at 400° and serve while hot. Slice.

FRUIT PUNCH

1 large can pineapple juice
2 C. boiling water
2 (3 oz. each) strawberry gelatin
6 C. cold water

½ C. sugar
1 can frozen orange juice
1 can frozen lemonade
1 qt. gingerale

Add boiling water to gelatin and sugar. Stir until dissolved. Add cold water and juices. Add gingerale just before serving.

124

CANDY

&

COOKIES

125

SCOTCH CHEWS

2 sticks butter
1 C. sugar
1 egg yolk
1 tsp. vanilla
1 C. cake flour

½ C. finely chopped nuts
1 C. flour
Egg white, beaten
¾ C. nuts

Cream butter; add sugar, egg yolk, vanilla and 1 C. cake flour. Add ½ C. nuts. Mix well. Add the second cup of flour. Mix all together. Spread in shallow pan (jelly roll) very tin. Cover with beaten egg white and the ¾ C. nuts. Bake 30 minutes at 375°.

BUTTERSCOTCH POWDERED SUGAR COOKIES

1 C. powdered sugar
½ C. butter
½ C. Crisco
1 egg
2 C. flour
1 tsp. soda

1 tsp. cream of tartar
½ tsp. salt
1 tsp. vanilla
1 C. chopped nuts
1 pkg. Nestle's butterscotch bits

Cream shortening and sugar; add eggs and vanilla. Add all dry ingredients. Add chips and nuts last. Spoon on greased cookie sheets. Bake in 375 degree oven till brown.

LEMONADE COOKIES

1 C. butter or margarine
1 C. sugar
2 eggs

1 tsp. baking soda
1 6-oz. can frozen lemonade (thaw)
3 C. pre-sifted flour

Preheat oven to 400°. In mixing bowl cream together butter and sugar. Add eggs, 1 at a time. Beat well after each. Combine flour and baking soda into egg mixture alternately with ½ C. lemonade concentrate. Drop by teaspoon 2'' apart onto ungreased baking sheets. Bake at 400° for about 8 minutes or till edges are browned slightly. Remove, brush lightly with remaining concentrate.

DREAM BARS

½ C. butter
½ C. brown sugar
½ to 1 C. flour
½ tsp. salt (optional)
1 C. brown sugar
½-1 C. coconut

2 eggs, well beaten
½ tsp. baking powder
¼-½ tsp. salt
1 tsp. vanilla
1 C. chopped pecans
2 T. flour

Cream butter, ½ C. brown sugar, ½ to 1 C. flour and salt. Pack into a buttered 8 x 8'' pan or 9 x 13'' pan (depending on how thick you want them). Bake 10-15 minutes in 350° oven. While this is baking, beat the eggs until frothy. Add the 1 C. brown sugar and beat until thick. Add the coconut which has been tossed with the 2 T. flour. Add chopped nuts, vanilla, salt and baking powder. Mix well. Spread over baked crust and bake 20 minutes at 350°. If desired, sprinkle with powdered sugar. Cut in bars while still warm. To make chocolate chip dream bars, substitute 1 C. chocolate chips for the coconut and nuts.

BURNT SUGAR COOKIES

1 C. sugar (burnt)
½ C. water
1 C. sugar
¾ C. lard
1 C. sour milk
    Drop and bake.

2 eggs
4½ C. flour
1 tsp. soda
1 tsp. baking powder

128

BREADS

RAISED DOUGHNUTS

1 C. milk
1 C. lukewarm water
⅔ C. sugar
2 tsp. vanilla
7 C. flour

1 pkg. yeast
½ C. shortening
2 eggs
1 tsp. salt

Scald milk and cool to lukewarm. Soften yeast in water and add milk. Cream shortening and sugar. Add eggs and beat and add vanilla. Add milk and yeast mixture, alternately with flour. Stir until smooth. Let rise until double in bulk, roll and cut; let rise until double in bulk. Fry and dip in glaze. Yields 50.

BUTTERSCOTCH ROLLS

1 pkg. yeast
1 box butterscotch pudding (not instant)
½ C. margarine
1 tsp. salt

¼ C. warm water
1½ C. milk
2 eggs
4½-5 C. flour

FILLING:
¼ C. butter or margarine
2 T. flour
⅓ C. pecans, chopped

⅔ C. brown sugar
⅔ C. coconut

Dissolve yeast in warm water. Combine pudding mix and milk. Cook until thick. Stir in margarine until melted. Cool to lukewarm. Add eggs, salt and yeast mixture. Stir in enough flour to make a stiff dough. Knead and place in greased bowl. Let rise until double. Divide dough into 3 parts. Roll each into a circle. Cut into wedges. Put 1 tsp. filling at wide end and roll toward point (as for butterhorns). Place on greased cookie sheet. Let rise until double. Bake at 350° until golden brown. Frost if desired.

EVAPORATED MILK COFFEE CAKE

½ C. shortening
2 C. sugar
4 tsp. baking powder
3 eggs
1 large can evaporated milk

½ C. butter
3 C. flour
1 tsp. salt
1 tsp. vanilla

Cream shortening, butter and sugar. Add eggs, 1 at a time, beating well after each addition. Sift together flour, baking powder and salt. Combine milk and vanilla. Add dry mixture and liquids alternately with sugar mixture. Pour slightly less than ½ batter into 9 x 13-inch greased and floured pan. Sprinkle with ½ cup sugar, ½ tsp. cinnamon and ½ cup nuts, chopped. Cover with remaining batter. Sprinkle 1/8 cup brown sugar, ¼ tsp. cinnamon and 1/8 cups nuts on top. Bake at 350° for 40 minutes.

COFFEE CAKE

1 pkg. yellow cake mix
1 pkg. instant pudding, coconut cream
1 tsp. vanilla
½ C. brown sugar
½ C. chopped pecans

1 C. sour cream
4 eggs
½ C. salad oil
¾ C. hot water
1½ tsp. cinnamon

Place cake mix, pudding mix, eggs, sour cream, salad oil and vanilla in a bowl; blend. Add hot water. Mix as you would a cake. Place one half of batter in lightly greased and floured 11 x 17-inch pan. Sprinkle with ½ combined mixture of brown sugar, cinnamon, and pecans. Pour rest of cake batter into pan and top with remainder of other mixture. Bake in 350° oven for about 35-40 minutes. Drizzle with powdered sugar glaze.

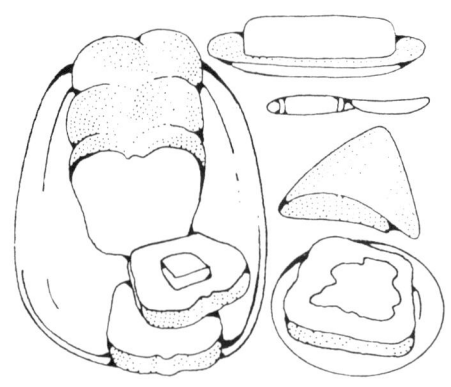

ORANGE BREAD

1 medium to large orange	1½ C. sugar
1 C. milk	1 egg
1 T. butter	2 C. flour
3 tsp. baking powder	1 tsp. salt

Put orange through grinder. Add a bit of water only if necessary and cook covered until rind is tender. Add sugar and cook to a thick syrup; cool. Add beaten egg, milk and butter. Add sifted flour, baking powder and salt. Makes 2 small loaves. Put in greased pan and bake 45 minutes to 1 hour in 350° oven.

PUMPKIN BREAD

⅔ C. oleo	3 C. sugar
4 eggs, beaten	⅔ C. water
2 C. pumpkin	1 tsp. vanilla
3⅓ C. flour	½ tsp. baking powder
2 tsp. baking soda	½ tsp. cinnamon
½ tsp. cloves	½ tsp. nutmeg
1 tsp. salt	

Cream oleo and sugar. Add eggs, pumpkin, water and vanilla. Sift all dry ingredients and add. Bake 1 hour at 350° in greased loaf pan.

CARROT BREAD

1½ C. grated carrots	1 C. sugar
¾ C. oil	2 eggs, beaten
1½ C. flour	½ tsp. salt
1 tsp. soda	1 tsp. cinnamon

Mix sugar, oil and eggs well. Add sifted dry ingredients and carrots alternately into egg mixture. Pour into greased and floured loaf pans and bake at 350° for 75 minutes. Makes two 7 x 3-inch pans or one 5½ x 9½-inch pan.

OATMEAL-GRAHAM BREAD

2 C. milk	1½ C. regular oatmeal
1 medium potato	2 tsp. brown sugar
½ C. granulated sugar	2 tsp. oleo
1 egg	2 T. dry yeast
½ C. lukewarm potato water	5 C. graham flour
1 tsp. salt	

Scald milk, while hot pour over oatmeal. Let stand until cool. Pare, cook and mash potato. Add brown sugar and oleo to potato while still hot. Let cool to lukewarm. Stir in unbeaten egg. Dissolve yeast in lukewarm potato water. Add to other mixture. Beat in 2 cups of graham flour. Let stand until light and bubbly, then add salt and 3 more cups of graham flour. Grease bowl and place in bowl. Cover and let rise until double in bulk. Makes 2 loaves. Bake 10 minutes at 400° and then 30 minutes at 350°.

VEGGIES

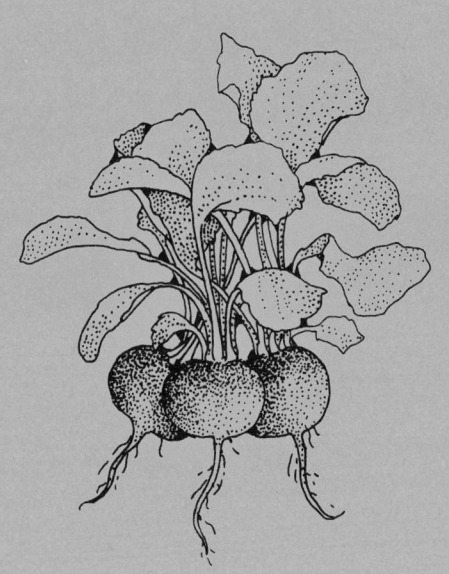

BECKETT'S AuGRATIN POTATOES

8 medium potatoes (peeled & sliced)
3 green peppers, chopped
3 medium onions, chopped

2 C. shredded sharp Cheddar
cheese or mild, if preferred
Salt & pepper, to taste

Spray roasting pan or casserole dish with Pam. Place a layer of sliced potatoes in pan, then ½ of pepper, onion, cheese, salt and pepper. Next another layer of potatoes, topped with the remaining peppers, onions, cheese, salt and pepper. Cover with remaining potatoes. Cover and bake at 350° for about 1½ hours or until tender.

SOUR CREAM SCALLOPED POTATOES AND HAM

2 slices smoked ham
8 medium potatoes (sliced thin)
1 can cream of mushroom soup
1 C. sour cream

1 tsp. salt
1 C. sliced onions
Dash of pepper
1 C. shredded Cheddar cheese

Cut ham into small pieces, slice potatoes. Combine soup, sour cream, salt and pepper. In greased 3 quart casserole alternate layers of ham and potatoes and onions with sour cream mixture. Top with shredded cheese. Cover casserole loosely with foil. Bake at 325° for 2½ hours.

QUICK POTATO CHEESE BAKE (Serves 8)

Instant mashed potatoes (8 servings)
½ C. grated Parmesan cheese
2 eggs
½ C. shredded Cheddar cheese

Prepare instant potatoes; add Parmesan cheese and eggs; beat until well blended. Spoon potatoes into 1½ quart casserole; sprinkle with Cheddar cheese. Bake at 350° fro 25 minutes or until slightly puffed and golden.

RICE WITH PARMESAN CHEESE

3 T. butter
¼ C. chopped onion
½ tsp. garlic powder
1 C. raw rice
1½ C. chicken broth
.Salt & pepper
2 or 3 T. grated Parmesan cheese

Melt 2 T. butter in heavy saucepan and add onion, stirring till onion wilts. Add rice and stir until a little brown; add broth, salt and pepper. Bring to boil and cover. Cook on low for about 20 minutes. Stir in remaining butter and cheese. About 4 servings. Good with fried chicken or fish dinner.

VEGETABLE BAKE

10½ oz. can cond. cream of mushroom soup
1 tsp. soy sauce
2 10-oz. pkg. frozen corn, green beans, lima
    beans or peas (cooked & drained)
⅓ C. milk
Dash of pepper
3½ oz. can French fried onions

In a 2½ quart casserole, combine soup, milk, soy sauce and pepper until smooth. Add the vegetables and half of then onions. Bake at 350° for 25 minutes. Top with remaining onions and bake an additional 5 minutes. Makes 6 servings.

RED CABBAGE

2 medium diced apples
Salt to taste
¾ C. sugar
1 T. rice (optional)

1 head red cabbage
¼ C. vinegar
3 T. butter or meat fryings

Cook 2 medium diced apples in a small amount of water for a couple of minutes. Add shredded cabbage and salt to taste. Cook covered for a few minutes. Then add large ¼ C. vinegar, ¾ C. sugar and butter or meat fryings, and rice. Continue cooking slowly, covered until done. Probably 15 to 20 minutes. The rice helps to thicken the juice. It shouldn't be too soupy. I do this "by guess and by gosh" so measurements may not be exact. Sort of depends of whether you have a large or small head of cabbage. This would be a large amount. Might be well to add vinegar and sugar to taste.

PARSNIP BALLS

1 pkg. parsnips
Salt

1 egg
Cracker crumbs

Peel and cut up parsnips. Boil until tender. Mash smooth. When cool, add egg and a pinch of salt. Add enough cracker crumbs to make firm balls. Roll in more crumbs and fry in deep fat.

CABBAGE CASSEROLE

20 crackers
1½ C. milk
¼ tsp. celery seed
3 T. butter

1 qt. shredded cabbage
1½ tsp. salt
¼ tsp. pepper

Crumble coarsely 10 crackers in a well greased casserole; add shredded cabbage and top with 10 more crumbled crackers. Heat milk, salt, celery seed, pepper and butter. Pour hot milk mixture over cabbage. Bake in moderate oven about 50 minutes. Dot with butter about 10 minutes before end of baking time. (May top with cheese.)

FIELD DAY BAKED BEANS (Serves 50-75)

3 gallon beans
1 large bottle Italian dressing
1 large bottle catsup
Beer as needed to keep moist

1 small jar mustard
3 medium onions (chopped)
1 lb. brown sugar

Bake 3-4 hours. (Rather than salad dressing and beer, you can use orange juice.)

SOUPER GREEN BEANS

1 qt. green beans (part drained)
1 can cream of mushroom soup
½ lb. bacon (fried, drained & crumbled)

6-8 slices American cheese
1 can French fried onion rings

Stir beans and soup together. Pour into 9 x 13-inch baking dish. Sprinkle with bacon, cover with cheese slices, then top with onion rings. Bake ½ hour at 350°.

SOUPS

&

SANDWICHES

RIGITONI STEW

2 cans tomato paste
5 cans water
Salt
Pepper
Parlsey flakes
Basil
Pinch of hot pepper seeds
Italian sausage

Bay leaf
Garlic
Onion
Oregano
Sweet pepper flakes
Leftover roast (beef or pork) or
   stew meat (cut in chunks)
Rigitoni noodles

Combine tomato paste, water and spices and simmer for 2-3 hours. Add leftover meat, or stew meat. Cut Italian sausage in small pieces and brown to remove the grease. Add this with everything above. Simmer another hour. Cook 1 box rigitoni noodles and add to the meat and sauce. Serve with tossed salad and hot bread.

MY FAVORITE PIZZA BURGERS

2 lb. ground beef
Salt
Chopped onion
1 small can mushrooms pieces (drained)

1 jar Pizza Quick sauce
Shredded mozzarella cheese
Steak or hamburger buns

Brown ground beef, seasoned with salt and chopped onion to taste; drain. Stir in mushroom pieces and Pizza Quick. Use meat mixtre to make open-faced sandwiches, using steak or hamburger buns. Top with shredded cheese. Place under broiler or in microwave to heat just until the cheese is melted. Serve immediately.

STUFFED PORK BURGERS DELUXE

1 lb. lean ground pork
1 C. soft bread crumbs
1 can (3 oz.) drained mushrooms

½ C. finely chopped onion
½ C. (2 oz.) shredded Swiss cheese

Combine ground pork and bread crumbs. Shape pork mixture into eight ¼" thick patties. In small bowl, combine mushrooms, onion and cheese. Spoon about ¼ C. mushroom mixture on four of the patties. Cover with remaining patties; press edges to seal. Place patties on rack in broiler pan. Broil at moderate temperature 3-4" from heat until browned, about 5 minutes. Turn and broil until patties are done, about 5 minutes. During last 2 minutes of broiling time, broil tomato slices alongside patties until heated through. Top each patty with broiled tomato slice. Season to taste with celery salt. Makes 4 servings.

HOME STYLE CHILI

1 lb. ground beef
1 can (1 lb. 13½-oz.) chili beans
1 can (15 oz.) chili beans
1 medium onion, chopped
1 qt. more or less tomato juice

1 green pepper, chopped
1 tsp. salt
3 tsp. chili powder
1/8 tsp. cinnamon, black pepper,
     nutmeg & clove

Brown beef, onion and pepper; drain. Add rest of ingredients and simmer for two hours. Add tomato juice and chili powder to desired thickness and taste.

CHEDDAR CHOWDER

2 C. boiling water
2 C. cubed potatoes
½ C. chopped carrots
½ C. sliced celery
¼ C. chopped onion
¼ tsp. pepper

¼ C. butter or margarine
¼ C. flour
2 C. milk
2 C. shredded Cheddar cheese
1 C. cubed ham

Combine water, vegetables and salt and pepper. Cover and simmer 10 minutes, or until vegetables are tender. Melt butter over medium heat. Blend in flour and add milk. Cook and stir until mixture is thickened and bubbly. Add cheese, stirring until melted. Add undrained vegetables and ham. Heat, but do not boil.

SALADS

PEA SALAD

1 16-oz. can peas (drained)
½ C. shredded sharp cheese
1/8 C. chopped onion
   Mix all ingredients together.

2 hard-boiled eggs
Salt & pepper, to taste
Salad dressing, to taste

POTATO SALAD

6 medium potatoes, boiled
4 hard boiled eggs
6 medium pickles
½ C. onion

2 T. sugar
2 T. mustard
Salt & pepper, to taste
Mayonnaise, to taste

   Chop potatoes and onion, dice or shred pickles. Add remaining ingredients and mix well.

MACARONI SALAD

1½ C. uncooked sea shell macaroni
¼ lb. Cheddar cheese, sharp
¼ C. pickles
2 T. chopped pimento

¼ C. onion
Salt & pepper, to taste
Mayonnaise, to taste

   Cook macaroni until tender. Add shredded cheese and shredded pickle. Mix well and add remaining ingredients.

147

FRENCH DRESSING

1 C. oil
¾ C. sugar
½ C. catsup
⅓ C. vinegar
　Blend or shake to mix.

1 tsp. paprika
1 T. lemon juice
1 clove crushed garlic or
　garlic salt, to taste

KAYE'S SALAD DRESSING

1 qt. Miracle Whip
⅔ C. sugar
2 tsp. celery seed
1 heaping T. prepared mustard

¼ C. sweet pickle relish
1 med. chopped onion (cut fine)
1/8 tsp. salt

　Combine ingredients and stir well until sugar is dissolved. Refrigerate and use as needed. I use this for potato salad, macaroni salad and kidney bean salad. Nice to have on hand for an emergency salad.

SPINACH VEGETABLE DIP

1 pkg. chopped frozen spinach
2 C. Hellman's mayonnaise
2 tsp. prepared mustard
½ C. minced onion

1 tsp. salt
1 tsp. pepper
2 T. parsley

　Thaw pkg. of spinach and squeeze out liquid. Mix all ingredients together. Good with cauliflower, carrots, celery and green pepper.

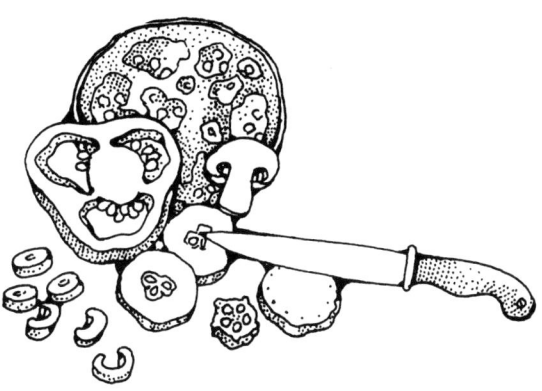

KRAUT SALAD

1 can kraut
½ C. green pepper, diced
½ C. chopped onion

½ C. diced celery
¼ C. diced pimento

DRESSING:
2 T. water
2 T. vegetable oil

⅓ C. vinegar
½ C. sugar

Combine first 5 ingredients. Mix well. Heat water, vinegar, oil and sugar. Pour over kraut and mix well. Chill.

DILLY SALAD DRESSING

1 C. low fat cottage cheese
2 T. skim milk
1 T. lemon juice

¼ tsp. salt
3 T. dill pickle relish
1 T. minced green onion

Place cottage cheese in small bowl. Beat on high speed of mixer until almost smooth, about 5 minutes. Stir in remaining ingredients. Chill 2 or 3 hours. Use over tossed salad.

SALAD DRESSING

½ C. water
½ C. vinegar
1 tsp. dry mustard
1 tsp. salt

¾ C. sugar
1 C. sour cream
1 T. flour
2 beaten eggs

Mix all together, then boil till thick, stirring constantly. Much easier to make in double boiler. Add pinch of cayenne pepper or paprika, if desired. Never had such a thing as commercial salad dressing when my mother started housekeeping. This is her recipe for salad dressing.

FROZEN CUCUMBER SALAD

12 C. cucumbers, sliced thin
  (peel if desired)
1 green or red pepper

4 stalks celery
1 large onion
Salt

SYRUP:
2¾ C. sugar

1 C. vinegar

  Sprinkle 4 T. salt over vegetables and stir. Let stand 4 hours. Bring sugar and vinegar to boil. Set aside and cool. Drain vegetables. Pour syrup over vegetables and let set overnight. May be frozen.

SPINACH SALAD

1 lb. fresh spinach
1 5-oz. can water chestnuts
  (drained & sliced)
1 can bean sprouts (drained)
  Mix above and toss with dressing.

2 hard-cooked eggs, sliced
6-8 slices bacon
  (fried crisp & crumbled)

DRESSING (Make Ahead):
1 C. oil
¼ C. vinegar
⅓ C. ketsup
  Serves 8.

1 medium onion
Salt & pepper, to taste
2 tsp. Worcestershire sauce

MAKE AHEAD SLAW

1 T. unflavored gelatine
¼ C. cold water
1 C. vinegar
2 C. sugar
1 tsp. celery seed
1 tsp. salt
¼ tsp. pepper

1 C. salad oil
8 C. shredded cabbage
3 carrots, grated
1 green pepper, diced fine
1 red pepper, diced fine
1 small onion, diced fine

Soften gelatine in cold water. Heat vinegar and sugar until dissolved. Add seasoning and stir in softened gelatine. Beat in salad oil and cool. Combine vegetables and toss with dressing. Refrigerate at least 24 hours. Add chopped celery if desired.

BEET SALAD

1½ C. chopped beets (cooked)
¾ C. beet juice
1 C. crushed pineapple

¾ C. pineapple or orange juice
1 T. sugar
1 pkg. lemon Jello

Boil beets and pineapple. Stir in juices and Jello. This is good served with fish or fowl.

GARDEN LETTUCE

Cut up a bowl of lettuce with scissors. Add three or four chopped green onions. Cook several slices of cut-up bacon. Then you may want to pour off some of the grease. Into a skillet (not too hot), break 3 or 4 eggs and stir around with fork. Let that cool a little. Break up in small pieces and put with lettuce.

DRESSING:

¾ C. sugar   ½ tsp. salt
¼ C. cream or milk   Dash of pepper
¼ C. vinegar

PARADISE CHICKEN SALAD

3½ C. cubed chicken or turkey   1 tsp. curry powder
   (leave pieces rather large)   1 C. grapes (seeded) or canned
¾ C. diced celery   ½ C. chunk pineapple
½ C. mayonnaise or salad dressing   1 small can mandarin oranges
2 T. chopped chutney   ½ C. flaked coconut

TOPPING:
Peanuts, almonds or sunflower seeds   Banana

Combine fruits, celery and chicken in a large bowl. In a small bowl, mix mayonnaise, chutney and curry powder. Cover and refrigerate. Just before serving drain any fruit juice from the large bowl. Toss with dressing. Over the top, sprinkle peanuts, almonds or sunflower seeds. Cut banana into long strips and arrange strips and several sections of mandarin oranges on the top of the salad.

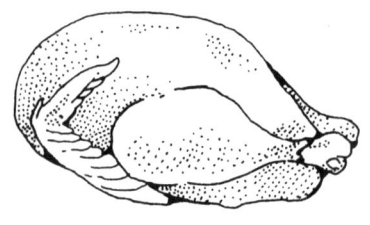

152

SALAD

1 can cherry pie filling
1 can crushed pineapple (drained)
  (same size as pie filling)

1 9-oz. container Cool Whip
Nuts (if desired)
1 can Eagle Brand milk

  Stir together and put in refrigerator. Better if sets awhile before using.

RASPBERRY APPLESAUCE SALAD

2 pkg. red raspberry Jello
1 No. 2 can applesauce

1 pkg. frozen red raspberries

TOPPING:
½ C. salad dressing

4 oz. pkg. cream cheese

  Prepare Jello as directed. Add raspberries and applesauce and set until firm.
Cream topping ingredients together until smooth. Spread over Jello mixture.

CHICKEN LOAF

1 chicken
Hard boiled eggs
Sliced olives
Pickles

Pimentos
Gelatin
1 pt. chicken broth

  Cook chicken until very tender, pick from bones and cut in small pieces. Place
a layer of chicken in a flat oiled pan, then a layer of eggs, olives, pickles and
pimentos. Top with a layer of chicken. Pour over the mixture ½ of a package of
gelatin which has been dissolved in a pint of chicken broth. When solid, cut into
squares.

PISTACHIO SALAD OR WATERGATE SALAD

1 9-oz. container Cool Whip
1 pkg. pistachio instant pudding
1 #2 can crushed pineapple
1 to 2 C. small marshmallows
½ C. chopped pecans
   Stir all together well. Refrigerate overnight.

PINEAPPLE SALAD

1 can pineapple chunks
2 C. small marshmallows
½ C. nuts
2 bananas

PUDDING MIXTURE:
½ C. sugar
3 T. flour
2 T. butter or oleo
1 egg
1 C. juice from pineapple
1 C. Cool Whip
   Take juice from pineapple; add water enough to make a cup. Cook pudding mixture and when cool fold in 1 C. Cool Whip and mix. Add bananas last.

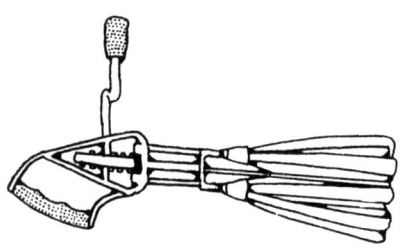

ORANGE SALAD

1 pt. cottage cheese (creamed style)
1 small pkg. orange Jello
1 C. mandarin oranges (drained)
9 oz. carton Cool Whip
   Sprinkle Jello over cheese and mix. Fold rest of ingredients into cheese mixture. Can substitute lime Jello and use with pineapple instead of mandarin oranges. Can serve at once or keep for several days. Serves 6.

MAIN DISHES

OLD FASIONED OYSTER DRESSING

Fowl giblets
2 qt. bread cubes
1 C. chopped celery
1 apple
2 T. or more minced onion

1 tsp. pepper
1 tsp. sage
2 eggs, beaten
1 pt. oysters, chopped

Cook giblets of fowl in 2 C. of more water. Cook celery, onion and apple separate from giblets. Then add to giblets. Pour over bread. Season with pepper and sage, then add eggs and oysters; mix well. Bake in moderate oven or stuff fowl.

QUICK LUNCH

1 can cream of mushroom soup
½ C. milk
Tuna

Canned peas
Pimento

Heat together and serve over biscuits.

RICE

1 C. rice   2 C. boiling water

In heavy skillet brown rice to the color desired (from very white to a toasty brown). Add boiling water gently and cover. Turn flame as low as possible and cook for 15-20 minutes. Leave lid on for 10-15 minutes longer (off flame). Remove lid and fluff the rice with a fork, put into a bowl and serve. Variations: Add pieces of chicken, fresh tomatoes, onions, mushrooms, herbs, beef boullion and etc.

ESCALLOPED CHICKEN

1 qt. coarsley cubed chicken
1 qt. broth (free from fat)

4 T. flour
4 T. chicken fat

DRESSING:
1½ qt. stale bread cubes
¾ C. butter (melted)
1¼ tsp. powdered sage
¼ C. cream or stock

¾ tsp. salt
2 T. chopped onion
Few grains peppers

Put 1½-inches layer of chicken in flat 9 x 13-inch pan. Cover with dressing lightly mixed. Mix broth, flour and chicken fat and bring to a boil. Pour gravy over dressing. Bake approximately 30 minutes or until lightly browned in 350° oven.

RICE O' BRIEN

1 C. white rice
2 C. rich chicken broth
1 tsp. Lawry's seasoned salt
Prestis Italian spices
¼ C. butter

½ C. slivered green pepper
½ C. chopped green onion
1 can mushrooms
3 T. diced pimento

Cook rice in broth with seasoned salt and spices to taste; drain. Melt butter and saute vegetables and rice until onion and pepper are tender crisp. Toss in pimentos and serve.

WESTERN CASSEROLE

1 lb. ground beef (lean)
1 can beans with chili
1 onion, chopped

Cheese
Corn chips

Brown onion and ground beef. Mix in the beans with chili. Put into a casserole dish and cover with a layer of your favorite cheese, then cover cheese with crushed corn chips. Bake uncovered in 350° oven for about 30 minutes.

TAMALE PIE

1 C. chopped onion
½ C. green pepper
1 lb. ground beef
1 15-oz. can tomato sauce
1 12-oz. can whole kernel corn, drained

½ tsp. salt
1 T. chili powder
Pepper
1½ C. shredded sharp Cheddar

CORN MEAL TOPPER:
¾ C. yellow corn meal
½ tsp. salt

2 C. cold water
1 T. butter or margarine

Cook onion, green pepper in a little hot fat until just tender. Add meat and brown lightly. Add next 6 ingredients. Simmer 20 to 25 minutes until thick. Add cheese; stir until melted. Pour into greased 10 x 6 x 1½-inch baking dish. To make corn meal topper; stir cornmeal and salt into cold water. Cook and stir until thick. Add butter and mix well. Spoon over hot meat mixture; smooth over the top. Bake in 375° oven, about 40 minutes. Makes 4-6 servings.

OVERNIGHT HAMBURGER CASSEROLE

1 lb. hamburger, uncooked
1 T. chopped onion
1 box or 1 C. uncooked macaroni
1 can tomato soup

1 can Cheddar cheese soup
2 tsp. sugar
1 tsp. salt
½ tsp. pepper

Combine all ingredients. Press into a 9 x 9-inch greased baking dish. Refrigerate several hours or overnight. Bake uncovered at 350° for 1 hour. May top with cheese, if desired.

LASAGNA

1 lb. hamburger
1/8 tsp. garlic salt
1 small onion
1 lb. can or 2 C. tomatoes
1 can (15 oz.) tomato sauce
1 tsp. sugar
1 T. Italian seasoning

1 pkg. (10 oz.) lasagna noodles
1 lb. cottage cheese
½ C. Parmesan cheese
2 beaten eggs
2 tsp. salt
½ tsp. pepper
Mozzarella cheese

Brown hamburger; add garlic salt and onion. Add tomatoes, tomato sauce, sugar and Italian seasoning. Simmer uncovered for at least 1 hour. Cook noodles according to directions on package. Combine cottage cheese, Parmesan cheese, eggs, salt and pepper. Mix well. Place layer of noodles in 9 x 13-inch pan. Spread with layer of cottage mix, then a layer of sliced or shedded mozzarella cheese, then a layer of meat sauce. Repeat layers. Bake at 375° for 30 minutes. Let stand a little while before slicing.

160

DEEP DISH PIZZA

1 can refrigerated biscuits (10-12)
¾ lb. hamburger
1 6-oz. can tomato paste
½ C. water
½ C. Cheddar or mozzarella cheese
  (I use more)

½ tsp. salt
½ tsp. oregano
¼ tsp. garlic powder
Pepper to taste
1 4-oz. can sliced mushrooms (opt.)

Preheat oven to 375°. Lightly grease 12-inch pie plate or cake pan. Line with biscuit dough, pressing it flat to form a crust. Brown hamburger in a skillet; add tomato paste, water, mushrooms and seasonings. Simmer on low heat for 10 minutes, stirring occasionally. Spread half the meat mixture over dough and top with half of cheese. Cover with remaining meat mixture, rest of cheese on top. Bake for 15 minutes, or until crust is golden brown and cheese melted. Can be prepared ahead, refrigerated or frozen and baked later.

ITALIAN DELIGHT

1 lb. hamburger
1 can Mexicorn
1 can tomato sauce
1 can tomato soup

½ lb. grated cheese
1 onion, chopped fine
½ lb. krinkled noodles

Brown meat and onion; add corn, soup and sauce. Make layer alternately-meat, cooked noodles and cheese. Bake at 350° for 15 minutes. Serves 6.

SUKIYAKI

WARISHITA:
1½ C. water & soup stock
½ C. soy sauce

½ C. mirin or sherry
2-3 T. sugar

4 eggs, or more
½ lb. shirataki or vermicelli (boiled in salted water, drained & cooled)
2 stick celery (cut diagonally)
6 oz. bamboo shoots (cut diagonally)

2 leeks, or scallion (cut diagonally)
8 fresh mushrooms
1-1½ lb. raw tender beef, slice thin
1 bunch Chrysanthemum leaves
1 black tofu (bean curd)

Bring warishita to a boil. In an electric frying pan or pan that can cook in middle of table fondue style, put a little lard and heat. Start cooking some of meat first; soon add some of warishita and plate of cut vegetables. Each portion should be removed and eaten as it is cooked and more added (fondue-like style). Cooked vegetables and meat are dipped into a beaten raw egg just before eating.

CORN BEEF AND MACARONI

1½ C. macaroni or 6 oz.
¼ lb. American cheese
1 can corn beef
1 can cream of chicken soup
Pepper

Buttered bread crumbs
½ C. onions (minced)
1 C. milk
1 tsp. salt

Cook macaroni, then drain and add other ingredients. Put in casserole and cover with bread crumbs. Bake at 350° for about 30 minutes or until brown on top. Serves 8.

162

BREAKFAST LASAGNA

8 to 10 slices white bread
2 lb. sausage (browned & drained)
8 oz. Cheddar cheese
8 eggs

2 C. milk
2 tsp. mustard
Salt
Pepper

Cube bread. In 9 x 13-inch pan, layer bread, sausage and cheese. Beat eggs and milk. Mix in mustard, salt and pepper. Pour over bread, meat and cheese. Cover and place in refrigerator at least 24 hours. Uncover and bake at 350° for 1 hour.

QUICK DEVILED CHICKEN

¼ C. butter
2 T. honey
¼ C. prepared mustard
1 tsp. curry powder

½ tsp. salt
2 large whole chicken breasts
  (skinned & halved)
2 T. sesame seeds

Heat oven to 375°. Place butter in 8-inch square Pyrex dish and put in oven a few minutes to melt. Remove dish from oven and stir in honey, mustard, curry powder and salt. Place chicken in dish, meaty side down. Bake 15 minutes, basting once. Turn chicken over, sprinkle with sesame seeds and bake 15 minutes longer or until tender, basting twice. Spoon remaining pan juice over chicken before serving.

163

ROCKY MOUNTAIN BRISKET WITH BARBEQUE SAUCE

1½ tsp. salt
1½ tsp. pepper
2 T. chili powder

1 tsp. crushed bay leaves
2 T. liquid smoke
4 lbs. beef brisket

Combine salt, pepper, chili powder and bay leaves. Rub meat completely with liquid smoke. Place meat, fat side up, in a large roasting pan. Sprinkle dry seasoning mixture on top. Cover tightly. Bake for four hours at 325°. Scraping off meat and cut in very thin slices across the grain. Serve with barbecue sauce. Makes 6 servings.

SAUCE:
3 T. brown sugar
1 14-oz. bottle catsup
½ C. water
2 T. liquid smoke
Salt & pepper, to taste

4 T. Worcestershire sauce
3 tsp. dry mustard
2 tsp. celery seed
6 T. butter
¼ tsp. cayenne pepper

Combine all sauce ingredients. Bring to a boil. Stirring occasionally. Cook for 10 minutes. Serve with sliced brisket. Note: Good by itself or in onion rolls.

SCALLOPED PINEAPPLE

2 sticks oleo
3 eggs, beaten
1 can crushed pineaple with juice

1½ C. sugar
4 C. cubed bread with crusts

Stir eggs, sugar and melted oleo together and add pineapple and bread. Bake 45 minutes at 350°. This can be fixed the night before and left in refrigerator until time to bake.

DESSERTS

STEAMED FRUIT PUDDING

½ C. chopped suet
⅓ C molasses
¼ C. white sugar
1 egg, well beaten
½ C. milk
1 tsp. cinnamon
1 tsp. soda
½ tsp. cloves

½ tsp. salt
1½ C. flour
½ C. figs
½ C. dates
1 C. nuts
1 C. raisins
Flour to coat fruit

Mix together suet, molasses, sugar, egg and milk. Stir in dry ingredients and mix well. Chop figs, dates and nuts. Add a little flour to coat figs, dates and nuts; stir in raisins. Fold fruit mixture into batter. Pour mixture into a well greased and floured colander. Place colander into a pan that has water coming just to the bottom of the colander. Steam 3 to 4 hours. While pudding is steaming check to make sure that the pan has ample water. Do not let pan cook dry. Remove pudding and serve with white sauce.

WHITE SAUCE:
1 C. sugar
4 T. flour
1½ C. boiling water

¼ C. butter
2 tsp. vanilla

Mix together in a saucepan sugar and flour. Stir in gradually the boiling water. Boil 1 minute, stirring constantly. Stir in butter and vanilla. Keep hot until time to serve.

ORANGE TAPIOCA PUDDING

1 pkg. orange tapioca pudding (or vanilla)
1 can pineapple tidbits
White grapes
Cool Whip

1 can fruit cocktail
1 can mandarin oranges
1 C. miniature marshmallows
Nuts

Drain fruit, use 1½ C. of juice to cook pudding. Stir constantly; cool. Fold in 1 container of Cool Whip and add fruit, marshmallows and nuts.

CHOCOLATE MARSHMALLOW DESSERT

1 pkg. Oreos
16 oz. marshmallows
1½ C. milk

1 lg. & 1 sm. carton Cool Whip
6 Hershey almond chocolate bars

Remove cream centers from Oreos and chop cookies in blender. Place in bottom of 9 x 13-inch pan (reserve ¼ C.). Melt marshmallows in milk over low heat. Cool completely. When marshmallow mixture is cool fold in Cool Whip. Chop candy bars and fold into the Cool Whip, marshmallow mixture. Pour over crumbs in pan and sprinkle with remaining crumbs. Refrigerate at least 6 hours.

RIBBON DESSERT

Graham crackers
2 pkg. red Jello
1 pkg. Dream Whip

Frosting (powdered sugar)
2 C. hot water
1 C. cold water

Line 9 x 9-inch with graham crackers. Add a layer of frosting and put another layer of graham crackers on top; chill. Dissolve 1 pkg. of red Jello in 1 C. of hot water, chill and add 1 pkg. of Dream Whip and beat. Pour over graham crackers and chill. Dissolve 1 pkg. of red Jello in 1 C. of hot water, add 1 C. of cold water and let thicken. Pour on top of other Jello mixture and chill until firm.

CHILDHOOD

Marion T. Justice

APPETIZERS

&

BEVERAGES

HORS D'OEUVRES - BACON ROLL-UPS

½ C. sour cream   ½ lb. bacon, cooked & crumbled
½ tsp. onion salt   1 8-oz. pkg. crescent rolls
    Separate rolls, mix the rest of the ingredients and spread on rolls. Cut each into thirds and roll up. Bake for 12-15 minutes at 375°.

BARBEQUED EGGS

6 hard boiled eggs (halved or sliced)   1 tsp. prepared mustard
1 C. catsup   1 T. horseradish (to taste)
½ C. brown sugar   ¼ stick butter or oleo
1 tsp. vinegar
    Combine barbeque sauce ingredients and boil slowly for five minutes to blend flavors and melt butter. Pour over eggs. Serve hot or cold. Tastes better than it looks or sounds.

CUCUMBER SANDWICH

1 8-oz. pkg. cream cheese   ½ tsp. Worcestershire sauce
1 pkg. dry Seasons Italian dressing   1 T. Miracle Whip
    Spread over slices of dark rye bread (use party bread, or cut slices in half). Top with slice of cucumber. Sprinkle dill weed on cucumber. Chill and serve.

HOT MOCHA MIX

1 C. unsweetened cocoa	2 C. sugar
4 C. non-fat dry milk powder	¾ C. instant coffee
1 vanilla bean or 3 T. dried orange peel	

Combine all ingredients and mix well. Store in airtight container for at least 1 week before using so that flavors can blend. To serve, stir well. Then place 3 T. of the mix in a cup and pour boiling water in, stirring as you go so that the mix dissolves nicely.

APRICOT NECTAR

1 (10 oz.) pkg. dried apricots	2 C. vodka
1 C. sugar	

Seal in jar, turn jar upside down each day for 3 weeks. Drain into decanter.

CHEESE BALL

2 jars Old English sharp cheese	½ tsp. onion or garlic salt
1 jar bacon, blue or pimento	1 tsp. Worcestershire sauce
1 3-oz. pkg. cream cheese	3 T. vinegar

Blend well and chill 1½ hours and roll in pecans or parsley flakes.

SPINACH DIP

2 10-oz. pkgs. frozen chopped spinach
1 C. sour cream
1 C. mayonnaise
¾ C. chopped green onion

1½ t. Beau Monde
1 tsp. dill weed
Salt & pepper

Thaw spinach and press very dry. Mix all ingredients in the blender or food processor until smooth.

CHEESE BALL

1 8-oz. pkg. cream cheese
1 glass Old English cheese
1 glass olive pimento cheese

1 glass Roka cheese
1 glass relish cheese

Have cheeses at room temperature. Combine 1 at a time, mixing after each addition and chill. Shape into balls. Roll in finely chopped peanuts covering thoroughly and refrigerate.

POLISH MISTAKES

1 lb. sausage (hot)
1 lb. sausage (mild)
1 C. chopped onion

1 T. Italian seasoning
2 lbs. Velveeta cheese
2 pkgs. party rye bread

Fry sausage until done - don't brown; drain. Mix onion, seasoning and cheese together and cook on low heat till cheese melts. Mix with sausage. Spread on bread, put on cookie sheet and freeze. Bake at 400° for 10 minutes.

175

PICKLED HAM

1 qt. diced ham
2 C. water

1½ C. vinegar
1 lg. onion (chopped)

Combine all ingredients and let stand overnight.

GARDEN CHEESE DIP

1 16-oz. small curd cottage cheese
1 3-oz. softened cream cheese
¼ C. minced onions with tops
¼ C. minced radishes

2 tsp. parsley, minced
1 small clove garlic, crushed
½ tsp. salt
Pepper to taste

Blend all ingredients. Cover and chill several hours or overnight. Makes 2⅓ cups.

CHEESE BALL

3 large pkg. cream cheese
2 small jars Old English sharp Cheddar

1 tsp. onion powder
2 T. Worcestershire sauce

Mix cheeses; add onion powder and Worcestershire sauce. Form into balls, refrigerate for 30-40 minutes. Roll in chopped nuts. May freeze, but thaw completely before serving.

CANDY

&

COOKIES

NELLE FARNAM

CHEESY APPLE 'N' OAT COOKIES

¾ C. sugar
½ C. butter
1 egg
1 tsp. vanilla
¾ C. sifted flour
½ tsp. baking powder

½ tsp. cinnamon
1½ C. oatmeal
1½ C. shredded cheese
1½ C. tart apples, finely chopped
1 tsp. salt

Cream sugar, butter, eggs and vanilla. Sift flour, baking powder, salt, cinnamon and add to creamed mixture. Stir in remaining ingredients. Drop by teaspoonfuls onto ungreased cookie sheet. Bake at 350° for 12 to 15 minutes or until golden brown. Makes 4 dozen cookies.

OATMEAL FUDGE BARS

½ C. soft shortening
1 C. brown sugar
1 egg
½ tsp. vanilla
¾ C. flour
½ tsp. soda
½ tsp. salt

2 C. oatmeal
1 6-oz. pkg. chocolate chips
1 T. butter or oleo
½ C. milk
¼ tsp. salt
1 tsp. vanilla
Nuts (optional)

Combine shortening, brown sugar, egg, ½ tsp. vanilla, dry ingredients (¾ C. flour, ½ tsp. soda and ½ tsp. salt) and oatmeal. Mix well. Save 1 cup of this mixture and press remainder into 9 x 9-inch pan. For the fudge layer cook chocolate chips, butter, milk and ¼ tsp. salt until butter and chips melt. Add vanilla and spread over oatmeal layer. Sprinkle with remaining oatmeal over the top. Bake 25 minutes at 350° or until surface is lightly browned. Cut into 24 bars.

OZARK BARS

1 stick oleo	3 tsp. vanilla
½ C. brown sugar	2 beaten eggs
½ C. white sugar	½ C. flour
½ C. brown syrup	½ tsp. baking soda
1 tsp. salt	

Cream oleo, brown sugar and white sugar. Add syrup, salt and vanilla. Beat and add eggs, flour, which has been mixed with the soda. Blend all together. Pour into buttered and floured 9 x 13-inch pan. Bake at 375° for about 30 minutes, until toothpick comes out clean. Cool and cut.

PINEAPPLE COOKIES

1 C. white sugar	2 tsp. baking powder
1 C. brown sugar	½ tsp. soda
1 C. shortening	½ tsp. salt
1 C. crushed pineapple	4 C. flour
1 tsp. vanilla	

Mix as given. Drop by teaspoon on greased cookie sheet. Can use juice from pineapple to make frosting. Bake at 350°.

RAISIN FILLED COOKIES

1 C. sugar	3½ C. flour
½ C. shortening	3 tsp. baking powder
1 beaten egg	½ C. sweet milk

Cream sugar and shortening then add egg and milk. Sift flour and baking powder twice then add to other ingredients. Roll out and cut cookies. Place a spoonful of the filling on a cookie then place another cookie on top and press the edges together. Bake in moderate oven.

FILLING:

¾ C. sugar	1 C. boiling water
1 T. flour	1 C. raisins

Cook all together until it thickens.

BREADS

5 O'CLOCK ROLLS

1 pkg. dry yeast	3 C. warm water
1 C. sugar	1 T. salt
¼ C. oil	2 eggs
8 C. flour (approx.)	

Mix and knead at 5 P.M. Knead at 6, 7, 8 and 9 P.M., (five times). At 9 o'clock, make into cinnamon rolls. Suggested base of 6 T. butter, ½ C. brown sugar, ½ C. corn syrup for each 9 x 13-inch pan. This recipe makes approximately 3 cake pans of buns or cinnamon rolls. Let stand on counter at room temperature overnight. Bake in pre-heated 350° oven for 15-20 minutes. Freezes well.

PECAN ROLLS

1 pkg. yeast	¼ C. water
1 C. milk	½ C. sugar
1 tsp. salt	⅓ C. butter or oleo
3 eggs	4-4½ C. flour

FILLING:

½ C. sugar	½ C. brown sugar
2 tsp. cinnamon	

TOPPING:

6 T. butter	6 T. corn syrup
Pecans	¾ C. brown sugar

Dissolve yeast in warm water. Scald milk and cool. Add other ingredients and knead to a smooth dough. Let rise and divide dough in half. Brush with melted butter and sprinkle with filling mixture. Combine topping and pecans in bottom of pan. Bake 25 minutes in 375° oven. Turn out immediately when done.

183

APPLE RAISIN LOAVES

3 eggs
2 C. chopped raw apples
1 tsp. vanilla
2 tsp. baking soda
1 tsp. salt
1 tsp. cloves

1½ C. oil
1½ C. sugar
3⅓ C. flour
1 tsp. baking powder
1 tsp. cinnamon
⅔ C. raisins

Heat oven to 350°. Grease and flour 2 loaf pans. Beat eggs, oil, apples, sugar and vanilla on low speed, 1 minute. Add flour, soda, baking powder, salt, cinnamon and cloves. Beat on low speed about 15 seconds. Beat on medium speed 45 seconds. Stir in nuts and raisins. Spread in pans. Bake 55 to 60 minutes or until done. Cool completely before slicing.

BANANA BREAD

½ C. shortening
2 eggs
2 C. flour
1 tsp. baking powder
½ C. chopped nutmeats

½ C. sugar
1 C. mashed bananas
½ tsp. soda
¼ tsp. salt

Mix and beat lightly. Bake in loaf pan at 350° for 40 minutes.

ZUCCHINI NUT BREAD

1 C. grated zucchini
1 egg
1½ C. flour
½ tsp. baking soda
¼ tsp. baking powder
½ tsp. salt

1 C. sugar
½ C. cooking oil
1 tsp. cinnamon
½ tsp. nutmeg
¼ lemon peel, finely shredded
½ C. chopped walnuts

In mixing bowl, beat together zucchini, sugar and egg. Add oil and mix well. Stir together flour, cinnamon, baking soda, nutmeg, baking powder, lemon peel and salt. Stir into zucchini mixture. Fold in walnuts. Pour into a greased loaf pan. Bake at 325° until done, about 60 to 65 minutes; remove from pan. Cool thoroughly on rack. Wrap and store overnight before slicing. Makes 1 loaf.

BUTTERHORNS

½ lb. butter or oleo
3 eggs
1½ C. warm milk
6 C. flour

⅔ C. sugar
1 pkg. yeast
1 tsp. salt

Cream butter and sugar. Add eggs, salt, ½ C. warm milk and 3 C. flour; beat. Stir yeast with 1 tsp. sugar and 1 C. milk. Let set for a few minutes then add to first mixture. By hand, add remaining 3 C. of flour and knead. Cover and refrigerate overnight. Remove the dough from refrigerator about ½ hour before shaping. Roll half of dough in shape of pie, spread with softened butter and cut into 16 wedges. Roll from large end into crescents and place on greased cookie sheet. Repeat with remaining dough. Let rise until doubled (about 3 hours). Bake for 15 minutes at 375° or until golden brown. If desired, frost with powdered sugar icing and sprinkle with nuts or coconut. (These freeze very well.) Makes 32.

GINGERBREAD

1 egg
1 C. sour cream
¼ tsp. salt
1¾ C. flour

1 C. sorghum
1 tsp. soda
Ginger
Cinnamon

Dissolve soda in a little hot water and combine with other ingredients. Bake at 350°. Serve warm with whipped cream.

COFFEE CAKE

1 pkg. coconut pecan frosting mix
1 C. sour cream
2 large chopped bananas

5 T. melted oleo
4 eggs
1 box yellow cake mix

Mix frosting mix and melted oleo; set aside. Beat together sour cream, eggs, 1 chopped banana and cake mix. Fold in other banana. Pour half batter in 9 x 13 inch pan. Top with half crumb mixture. Add rest of batter and rest of crumbs. Bake at 350° for 30-40 minutes.

ST. PETER BREAD

½ C. warm water
2 C. scalded milk
½ C. brown sugar
1 T. salt

1 pkg. yeast
2 C. oats
2 T. shortening
5-6 C. flour

Scald milk; add oats, brown sugar, shortening and salt; cool to lukewarm. Dissolve yeast in water; add to milk mixture. Mix in flour in two addition; mix well. Turn onto lightly floured board; cover and let rest 10 minutes. Knead until smooth and elastic; round up in greased bowl; bring greased side up. Let rise till double (1½-2 hours). Punch down, divide and shape into loaves or braids (4 loaves). Roll lightly on surface sprinkled with oats, sesame seeds or poppy seeds. Place in greased pans and cover. Let rise until double. Bake at 375° for 30-40 minutes.

RAISIN OATMEAL BREAD

2 pkg. yeast
1½ C. milk
¼ C. shortening
1 egg
1 C. raisins

½ C. warm water
⅓ C. sugar
2 tsp. salt
1 C. quick oats
5½-6 C. flour

Soak yeast in warm water. Heat milk and add sugar, shortening, salt and egg. Cool until lukewarm and add yeast mixture. Add raisins, slowly add flour. Mix in enough flour to be able to handle dough easily. Turn onto a floured surface and knead about 10 minutes. Place in greased bowl, grease top and let rise in warm place until double, about 1 hour. Punch down and divide in half. Roll each half into rectangle, butter surface and sprinkle with ½ cup sugar, mixed with 1 T. cinnamon. Roll up and place in buttered loaf pan and let rise until dough is doubled. Bake at 375° for about 40 minutes. Loaves can be glazed with powdered sugar and cream or eaten just sliced.

VEGGIES

KRAUT AND TOMATOES

1 can kraut
1 can tomatoes
2 slices bacon
1 small onion
1 C. brown sugar

    Fry bacon, drain all but 1 T. of grease. Cut bacon in pieces. Add other ingredients and bake for 1 hour at 350°. Cover with foil.

SOUR CREAM POTATOES

8 med. potatoes
    Boil till soft. Mash with milk, butter, and 1 pt. of sour cream, salt and pepper. Add Lawrey's seasoned salt, til slightly orange cast. Bake at 350° for ½ to 1 hour.

VEGETABLE CASSEROLE

1 pkg. frozen broccoli
1 pkg. frozen brussels sprouts
1 pkg. frozen cauliflower
1 can mushrooms (drained)
1 can mushroom soup
1 small jar Cheez Whiz

    Cook vegetables 4 minutes and drain. Heat soup and cheese. Pour over vegetables. Sprinkle croutons, potato chips, or bread crumbs over the top. Bake for 30 minutes.

GREEN RICE CASSEROLE

1 pkg. frozen broccoli
1 jar Cheez Whiz
1 can cream of chicken soup
1 7-oz. pkg. minute rice

1 stick margarine
1 soup can milk or
Half & Half

Prepare rice and boil broccoli. Combine all ingredients in a large baking dish and stir until well mixed. Bake at 350° for 45 minutes. You may substitute cream of mushroom, cream of celery or any cream soup depending on your taste. If so desired, 1 onion may be chopped and cooked with broccoli.

POTATOES ROMANOFF

6 large potatoes
2 C. large curd cottage cheese
1 C. dairy sour cream
1-2 cloves garlic
Paprika

1 tsp. salt
¼ tsp. pepper
2-3 chopped green onions
1 C. shredded Cheddar cheese

The potatoes should be boiled until they are just barely tender, but yet soft. Cut them up into small cubes and combine them with the cottage cheese, sour cream, garlic, salt, pepper and green onion. Turn the mixture into a buttered casserole and sprinkle with shredded cheese. Add a little paprika, if desired. Bake at 350° for 25-30 minutes.

ONION RINGS

1 C. flour
½ tsp. salt
½ C. evaporated milk
2 large onions

2 T. salad oil
1 egg white
6 T. water

Mix milk, egg and salad oil. Pour into flour and salt. Add water until batter is of medium consistency. Fry at 350°, turning once.

CONNECTICUT CORN PUDDING

6 strips bacon (fried crisp)
½ green pepper, diced
1 small onion, diced
2 C. corn (fresh, frozen or canned)
½ C. soft bread crumbs

2 eggs, beaten
2 C. top milk
1 tsp. salt
½ C. buttered crumbs

Drain bacon on a paper towel. Saute pepper and onion in 2 T. of the bacon drippings. Add corn, bread crumbs, eggs, milk, salt and bacon. Stir together. Pour into a greased 1½ quart casserole. Top with buttered crumbs. Bake at 375° for 40 minutes.

GREEN BEAN - WATER CHESTNUT BAKE

1 medium onion, diced
1 4-oz. can mushrooms pieces
¼ C. margarine
¼ C. flour
1 pint ½ & ½
1/8 tsp. Tabasco sauce

1 tsp. salt
½ tsp. pepper
½ tsp. butter flavoring
2 cans French cut green beans
1 can water chestnuts
1 C. grated cheese

Saute onion and mushrooms in the margarine. Stir in flour. Add all but the last three ingredients and stir until thick. Gently add beans and chestnuts. Pour into greased casserole, sprinkle with cheese and bake at 350° for about 30 minutes.

CALICO BEANS

1 can butter beans
1 can pork & beans
½ C. ketchup
½ lb. hamburger, browned
Salt & pepper, to taste

1 can kidney beans
½ C. brown sugar
4 or 5 strips bacon (fried & drained)
Onion, if desired

Bake in 350° oven for 1 hour.

CAULIFLOWER BROCCOLI AU GRATIN

10 oz. each frozen or fresh veg.
   (cauliflower & broccoli)
2 C. hot milk
2 T. butter
¼ C. chopped onion

2 oz. jar drained pimento
1½ T. flour
¼ tsp. salt & pepper
¾ C. grated cheese
10 soda crackers

Cook vegetables as directed; drain. Put in 2 quart casserole. Make white sauce with milk, butter and flour. Sprinkle onion, pimento and cheese over vegetables. Pour sauce over all. Sprinkle with crackers and paprika. Bake at 350° for 45 minutes.

SOUPS

&

SANDWICHES

TOASTY HOT DOG ROLL-UPS

2 C. water
8 frankfurters
½ C. butter or margarine (1 stick)
8 slices white bread

2 tsp. prepared mustard
4 slices process American cheese
Catsup

Heat oven to 375°. Heat 2 C. of water to boiling in medium saucepan over medium heat. Carefully drop 8 frankfurters into the water. Reduce heat. Cover and simmer over low heat 5 to 8 minutes. Melt ½ C. butter in small saucepan over low heat. Place 8 slices bread on ungreased cookie sheet. Brush the top sides of the slices with about half of the melted butter. Spread with 2 tsp. mustard (about ¼ tsp. for each slice). Cut 4 slices cheese diagonally in half so you have 8 cheese triangles. Top each bread slice with 1 cheese triangle. Place one frankfurter on top of each cheese triangle with tongs. Fold the bread over to make a triangle shape. Fasten with 2 wooden picks, 1 on each side, poking them through the bread and frankfurters. Brush the outside of the bread triangles with remaining melted butter. Bake in 375° oven for 10 to 15 minutes or until golden brown. Serve with catsup. Note: In place of the mustard, you can spread the buttered bread with 2 tsp. horseradish or pickle relish.

PARTY PUPS

2 lbs. ground beef
¼ C. milk
1 egg
1 roll Ritz crackers (crushed)
Celery salt

Garlic salt
Onion salt
Lawry's seasoning salt
1 T. minced onion
1 T. water

Mix first four ingredients. Soak seasonings in water. Shape into oblong balls and wrap with a strip of bacon and grill 15 minutes.

LARGE QUANTITY CHILI CON CARNE

4 cans (No. 2) red kidney beans
4 cans (No. 2) red chili style beans
5 lbs. ground beef
1 C. chopped onions
1 C. fat

1½ qt. tomato puree
½ C. flour
½ C. water
2 T. salt

Brown meat and onion in fat. Add tomato puree and simmer until beef is tender. Make a paste of flour and water and add to beef mixture, stirring constantly. Add beans and seasonings and cook until flavors are well blended. More chili powder can be added if desired.

CHICKEN-CHEESE SOUP

2 whole chickens
16 C. seasoned water
10 chicken boullion cubes
2 C. shredded carrots
1½ C. chopped celery
½ C. minced onion

2 C. uncooked rice
1 T. parsley flakes
1 10-oz. can tomatoes & chilies
2 lb. Velveeta cheese
3-5 T. cornstarch

Cook chicken in the 16 C. water until done. After this has cooked down; add enough more water to cover the chicken. Remove the chicken from broth. Add boullion cubes, carrots, celery, onion, rice, parsley flakes, tomatoes and chilies. Simmer until vegetables and rice are done. Add cheese and cornstarch, salt and pepper to taste. Take chicken off bone and put back in the soup.

OYSTER STEW

1½ gallon (whole) milk
½ pt. cream of 2 half pts. of ½ & ½

½ stick of butter, to simmer
1 pt. or 12 oz. of oysters

This amount depends on how many eats them and how rich you want them. 1½ pints would be best. Season to taste. I always simmer my oysters. Serves 30-35 people.

SALADS

CRUNCHY VEGETABLE SALAD

1 C. vegetable oil
1 C. sugar
½ C. vinegar
2 C. small English peas
2 C. cut green beans, drained

1 can water chestnuts, sliced
4 large ribs celery, chopped
1 4-oz. can chopped pimentos
Salt to taste
Mushrooms or cocktail onions, opt.

Mix oil, sugar and vinegar until blended. Add remaining ingredients and marinate overnight. Do not omit water chestnuts as they add a very definite taste to this salad. The salad keeps well for several days, but is best when it has marinated at least 8 hours.

PICNIC SALAD

2 cans drained green beans
1 can drained sliced carrots
4 stalks celery (cut in ½-inch slices)

½ green pepper (cut in half rings)
1 4-oz. can pimentos (drain & chop)
1 sweet onion (cut in rings)

DRESSING:
2 C. vinegar
1½ C. sugar

1 tsp. salt
Dash garlic salt

Combine vegetables in bowl with a cover. Heat the dressing ingredients until the sugar dissolves. Pour hot dressing over the vegetables. Cover and chill. This will keep for weeks in refrigerator.

DRESSING FOR LETTUCE SALADS

¾ C. mayonnaise
2 T. honey
    Mix and coat lettuce salad.

1 T. lemon juice
1 T. caraway seeds

ROTONI SALAD

8 oz. Rotoni macaroni
1½ C. vinegar
1½ C. sugar
1 tsp. parsley flakes
1 tsp. Accent
1 tsp. garlic powder
2 tsp. prepared mustard

1 C. green pepper (chopped)
1 C. celery (chopped)
½ C. carrot (grated)
½ C. chopped cucumber (optional)
½ tsp. salt
¼ C. oil

    Cook rotoni for about 15 minutes. Drain and rinse. Add rest of ingredients.

FRUIT DIP

1 8-oz. pkg. cream cheese (soft)
½ C. brown sugar

¼ C. powdered sugar
1 tsp. vanilla

    Beat together with electric mixer. Better is made day before serving. Especially good with apple slices.

VEGETABLE SALAD

1 pkg. lemon Jello
½ C. sugar
1 C. hot water
¼ tsp. salt
½ C. cold water

2 tsp. vanilla
½ C. salad dressing
1½ C. shredded cabbage
1 carrot, shredded
1 C. celery, chopped

Combine Jello, sugar, hot water, salt, cold water and vanilla and let set until it begins to gel. Beat it up and add salad dressing. Then add vegetable ingredients. Chop up a little red or green pepper and 2 tsp. grated onion and add to other ingredients. Can double for larger pan.

BLUE CHEESE OR ROQUEFORT DRESSING

1 C. evaporated milk
½ C. salad oil
¼ C. vinegar

½ tsp. salt
Dash garlic powder
½ C. crumbled blue or Roquefort
  cheese

Mix all with mixer.

POPPY SEED DRESSING

½ C. honey
½ C. salad oil
1 tsp. salt

1 tsp. vinegar
4 tsp. poppy seeds

Mix well and store in refrigerator.

LOW CALORIE MOCK POTATO SALAD

1 head cauliflower
2 oz. chopped onion
2 oz. chopped celery
2 T. pickle relish

1 T. mustard
4 T. diet or reg. mayonnaise
½ T. parsley flakes

Clean cauliflower and cook until tender. Mix all ingredients. Makes 4 servings.

THREE-BEAN SALAD

¼ C. chopped onion
1 can cut green beans

1 can cut yellow wax beans
1 can red kidney beans

Drain all vegetables.

DRESSING:
½ C. salad oil
½ C. vinegar
¾ C. sugar

½ tsp. salt
½ tsp. pepper

Pour dressing over vegetables and stir frequently. Let stand and refrigerate overnight.

SUPER SALAD

1 bunch fresh broccoli
1 bunch green onions
1 lb. fresh mushrooms

Cherry tomatoes
1 jar Wishbone Italian dressing

Slice first 3 items. Cut cherry tomatoes in half, add to sliced vegetables. Pour over all this the Italian dressing. Marinate 8 hours.

CUCUMBER SALAD

4 unpeeled cucumbers   1 large onion, sliced

DRESSING:
½ C. sugar   1½ C. mayonnaise
Salt & pepper   Vinegar (enough to make creamy)
    Pour dressing over cucumbers and onions. Refrigerate overnight.

LAYERED LETTUCE SALAD

    1 medium head lettuce, cut to bite size. Put in bottom of 9 x 13-inch pan. Chop 1 C. celery and put over lettuce, (I omit the celery). Add 10 oz. pkg. frozen peas over celery and lettuce. Chop ½ C. onion and 4 hard boiled eggs; add to above. Crisp and crumbled 8 slices bacon and add. Mix 2 C. Miracle Whip and 2 T. sugar. Spread evenly over top of mixture. Grate and spread over the top 4 ozs. Cheddar cheese. Do not stir. Will keep 2 weeks.

TEX MEX (Taco) SALAD

Makes 6 Layers:
1. Mound 2 cans bean dip in center of plate or tray.
2. Three mashed avocados.
3. Mixture: 1 C. sour cream, ⅓ C. mayonnaise, 1 pkg. taco seasoning.
4. Two medium tomatoes, chopped.
5. Sliced or chopped black olives.
6. 6 or 8 oz. grated cheese, Cheddar or Monterey Jack.

HOLIDAY SALAD

PART 1:
1 small pkg. cherry Jello
   Dissolve Jello in 1 C. hot water and then add 1 C. cold water. Let cool until it starts to congeal.

PART 2:
1 small pkg. lime Jello   20 large marshmallows
2 C. pineapple juice
   Heat pineapple juice and dissolve Jello in this, then add marshmallows. Let cool, until it starts to congeal and whip.

PART 3:
   Combine 1 3-oz. pkg. Phil. cream cheese with ⅔ C. chilled evaporated milk. Whip and add 1 C. less 2 T. Miracle Whip. Add ¼ C. drained, crushed pineapple. Add this mixture to the lime Jello mixture. Arrange the Jello so red Jello will be on top when served. I double the recipe and put in a round Jello mold.

CHINESE BEEF SALAD

2 C. cubed cooked roast beef   ½ C. chopped onion
1 C. shredded raw carrot   ⅔ C. salad dressing
1 C. diced celery   Seasoning salt, to taste
½ C. diced green pepper   1 can (3 oz.) chow mein noodles
   Combine all ingredients, except chow mein noodles and mix well; chill. Add chow mein noodles just before serving. Serves 6-8 as a main dish.

FRESH FRUIT SALAD

1 tall can pineapple tidbits (drained)   2 C. white grapes
2 C. miniature marshmallows   1 cantaloupe (balled)

DRESSING:
1½ C. pineapple juice (or other fruit juice)   ½ C. sugar
1 egg   2 T. cornstarch
   Cook dressing until thick. Cool and add to fruit.

COOL STRAWBERRY SALAD

8 oz. pkg. cream cheese   1 box strawberries
9 oz. container Cool Whip   1 C. sugar
   Mix cream cheese and sugar well. Add Cool Whip and strawberries. (If berries are really juicy, don't put all of the juice in.)

FIVE-CUP SALAD

1 C. cooked rice   1 C. crushed pineapple
1 C. miniature marshmallows   1 C. nuts
1 C. whipped cream
   Mix, chill and serve.

PINEAPPLE CHEESE SALAD

1 egg
⅓ C. sugar
2 T. flour
1 can pineapple (drained & save juice)

½ lb. diced cheese
18 marshmallows

Make dressing of egg, sugar, flour and juice from pineapple. Let cool, then add cheese, pineapple and diced marshmallows.

PEACH SALAD

1 3-oz. box peach Jello (dry)
1 small carton cottage cheese

9 oz. carton Cool Whip
1 can peaches (drained)

Cut peaches in bite sizes. Mix with Jello and cottage cheese. Last, fold in Cool Whip.

CHRISTMAS SALAD

1 box strawberry Jello
1 box lime Jello
1 box lemon Jello
1 box orange Jello

Chunk pineapple
Mandarin oranges
Whipping cream or
Cool Whip

Combine all these each in separate bowls with boiling water, as directed on box. Set aside to firm up. (Usually the day before.) In a large bowl add all sorts of fruits, well drained, small marshmallows and bananas. Cube Jello by cutting across several ways while in the bowls. Add all but a small amount (reserved for the top) to the fruit. Add whipping cream or Cool Whip. Top with the last of Jello to brighten the dish. This is an old time favorite of the family passed along.

MAIN DISHES

CHICKEN OF THE SEA TUNA FLORENTINE

2 pkg. (10 oz. each) frozen chopped
spinach (thawed)
2 T. instant minced onion
1 can (12½-oz.) chicken of the sea
tuna (drained)
6 hard cooked eggs (sliced)

2 cans (10¾ oz.) cond. cream
mushroom soup
1 C. (½ pt.) sour cream
Salt & pepper
¼ C. melted butter
2 C. soft bread crumbs (4 slices)

Squeeze spinach to remove excess liquid. Spread spinach evenly in grease 2 quart casserole. Sprinkle with onion, tuna and eggs. Mix mushroom soup and sour cream. Pour mixture evenly over eggs. Mix melted butter and crumbs and sprinkle evenly over top of casserole. Bake in preheated moderate oven (350°) for 30-35 minutes or until golden brown and bubbly. Serves 6.

STUFFED PEPPERS

6 medium green peppers
2 small cans shrimp (hamburger or
ground pork may be used)
2 C. cooked rice (salted)
1 C. salad dressing

2 T. chopped onion
Dash of Tabasco sauce
1 8-oz. can seasoned tomato sauce
(I use kind with meat in)

Cut off tops of peppers. Clean and pre-cook 5 minutes in salted water; drain. Combine next 4 ingredients. Add Tabasco sauce. Fill peppers. Set upright in casserole. Pour tomato sauce around the peppers. Bake at 350° for 30 minutes. Spoon sauce over peppers as you serve or eat them. Very good.

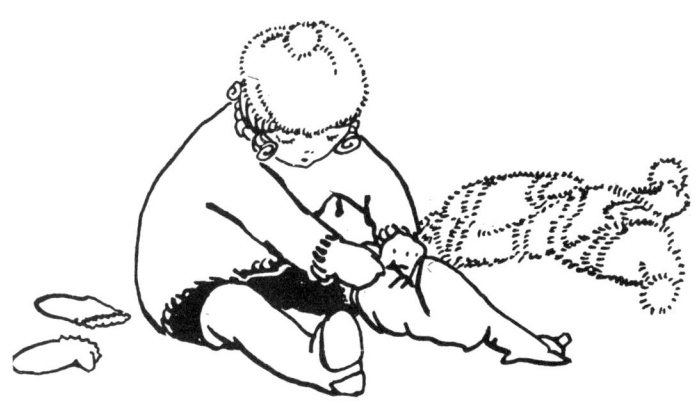

WILD RICE CASSEROLE

2 C. boiling water
⅔ C. wild rice
1 can chicken rice soup
1 small can mushroom pieces
½ C. water
1 tsp. salt
1/8 tsp. celery salt
1/8 tsp. onion salt

1/8 tsp. garlic salt
1/8 tsp. paprika
1/8 tsp. liquid smoke or
   hickory seasoning
1/8 tsp. pepper
1 small bay leaf, crumbled
3 T. chopped onion
3 T. bacon drippings or oil
½ lb. ground beef

Pour boiling water over wild rice. Cover and let stand 15 minutes; drain. Add chicken soup, mushrooms (and liquid), ½ C. water and seasonings. Saute onions in bacon drippings until slightly browned, then add ground beef; stir until brown and crumbly. Mix into rice and pour into casserole. Bake in slow oven (325°) for one hour. Grated cheese may be sprinkled over the top of mixture before baking. Serves 4 easily.

HOT CHICKEN SALAD

2 C. cooked, cut-up chicken
1 C. Miracle Whip
2 T. instant onion flakes
Pinch of curry powder
2 C. celery (chopped fine)

2 T. lemon juice or real lemon
2 C. seasoned croutons
1 C. shredded cheese
   (Cheddar is good)

Mix lightly - don't press down. Cover and bake at 350° for about 30 minutes. Uncover and bake about 8 minutes more.

CHICKEN-RICE PILAF

1 C. regular rice
1 tsp. curry powder
Salt & pepper, to taste

1 3# chicken (cut-up)
1 can mushroom soup
1 C. water

Grease a 9 x 13-inch pan. Put rice in the bottom of the pan. Arrange chicken pieces over top. Mix remaining ingredients together and pour over chicken. Bake at 350° until tender. Bake covered with foil.

CHICKEN ENCHILADAS CASSEROLE

1 chicken
1 green pepper
1 onion
1 can chopped green chilies

Flour tortillas
Mild Cheddar cheese
1 can cream of chicken soup
1 8-oz. container sour cream

Boil and debone chicken; save broth. Saute green pepper and onion, then add green chilies. Combine chicken and sauted mixture. Line 9 x 13-inch pan with tortillas (dip tortillas in oil first). Cover tortillas with chicken mixture. Cover with cheese (grated). Repeat tortilla, chicken, cheese layers. Mix 1 can cream of chicken soup, 1 can broth and 1 C. sour cream. Pour over casserole. Bake 30 minutes at 350°, uncovered.

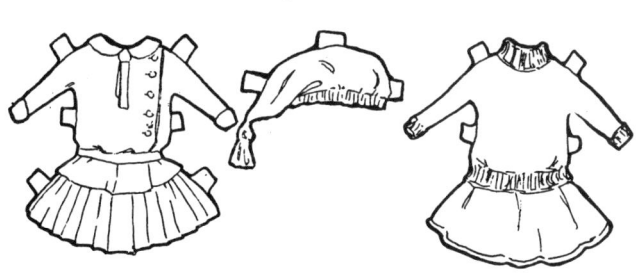

CHICKEN CASSEROLE

2 C. cooked diced chicken
2 C. uncooked macaroni
2 10½-oz. cans mushroom soup
1 soup can of milk
13¾-oz. chicken broth
1 small onion, chopped fine

½ green pepper, chopped fine
1 2-oz. jar pimento, sliced
½ lb. grated Cheddar cheese
½ tsp. salt
5 oz. jar water chestnuts (sliced)

Combine the above and mix well. Pour into greased 9 x 13-inch baking dish. Cover with foil and refrigerate overnight. Remove foil and bake at 350° for 1 hour.

PIZZA CASSEROLE

1 lb. ground pork	1 can tomato soup
⅓ C. chopped onion	⅓ C. water
1 tsp. oregano	2 C. cooked noodles
½ tsp. salt	½ C. shredded cheese

Cook pork, onion and seasonings in skillet until pork in brown. Add soup, water and noodles. Spoon into greased casserole dish. Sprinkle cheese on top. Bake at 350° for 30 minutes. Crushed cheese crackers may be sprinkled over the top before baking.

SHIPWRECK

2 T. cooking oil	1 can red kidney beans
1 layer potatoes, thinly sliced	1 can tomato sauce
1 lb. hamburger	

Put oil in baking dish. Add layer of sliced potatoes, hamburger, beans, salt and pepper. Pour tomato sauce over all. Bake at 350° for 1 hour. To microwave, omit oil. Cook at full power for 25-30 minutes, turning occasionally.

IMPOSSIBLE CHEESEBURGER PIE (6 to 8 Servings)

1 lb. ground beef	1½ C. chopped onion
½ tsp. salt	¼ tsp. pepper
1 C. Cheddar cheese	1½ C. milk
¾ C. Bisquick	3 eggs

Cook and stir beef and onion until brown; drain. Stir in salt and pepper. Spread in lightly greased 10'' pie plate; sprinkle with cheese. Beat remaining ingredients until smooth. Pour into pie plate. Bake until golden brown and knife inserted in center comes out clean, about 30 minutes. Let stand 5 minutes before cutting. If using 9'' pie plate, decrease milk to 1 cup, baking mix to ½ C. and eggs to two.

HAMBURGER CASSEROLE

1 lb. hamburger	1 can cream soup (chicken, celery
1 small onion or onion flakes	or mushroom)
1 pkg. mixed vegetables	1 C. milk
1 box tater tots	

Lightly brown hamburger and onions. Season to taste. Layer in casserole dish with meat mixture first, next vegetables and then tater tots on top. Combine soup and milk and pour over all. Bake 350° for 1 hour. Chopped celery and green pepper may also be used. Also sliced potatoes, but par-boil for 6-8 minutes and all the soup last over all. Makes 6 servings. Can be frozen or just refrigerated and baked later.

SWISS SCRAMBLED EGGS

1 C. soft bread crumbs (no crust)
1¾ C. milk
8 eggs, slightly beaten
Salt & pepper, to taste

¼ C. margarine
¼ lb. sliced Swiss cheese
8 slices bacon (fry crisp & crumble)
½ C. Contadina dry bread crumbs

Soak soft bread crumbs in milk. Drain after 5 minutes, saving milk. Combine and whip eggs, salt, pepper and milk, saved from bread crumbs. Melt 2 T. of margarine and scramble egg mixture, only until soft cooked. Add soaked bread. Place in buttered 9-inch square casserole. Arrange on top single layer of Swiss cheese. Melt remaining margarine with the dry bread crumbs and sprinkle over cheese. Sprinkle crumbled bacon on top. Bake in 400° oven for 5 minutes, or until cheese bubbles. If made the day before, set out early to get room temperature. Bake in 350° oven for 15 minutes. Note: To serve 8 to 10 people, I added one more cup bread crumbs, 2 C. milk (total) and two more eggs. Otherwise the same.

CHIPPED BEEF CASSEROLE

1 C. macaroni, uncooked
1 can mushroom or chicken soup
1 C. milk
1 C. sharp Cheddar cheese

1 C. chipped beef
¼ C. onion (optional)
2 hard boiled eggs (optional)

Place macaroni in buttered baking dish. Combine soup, milk, shredded cheese, chipped beef (snipped fine), and onion (minced). Pour over macaroni. Do not stir. May garnish with the sliced eggs. Cover and refrigerate 6 to 8 hours or overnight. When ready to bake take a spoon and go to the bottom of casserole in several places, without stirring. Bake at 350° for 1 hour.

HAM AND EGG BRUNCH

8 or 9 bread slices (cubed)
1 lb. ham, diced
½ lb. Old English cheese (cubed)
3 eggs, beaten

2 C. milk
½ tsp. dry mustard
½ tsp. salt
¼ lb. melted butter

Cube 6 or 7 of the bread slices and place in 9 x 12-inch cake pan (greased). Mix ham and cheese and spread on bread layer. Mix eggs, milk, mustard and salt and pour over ham and cheese. Cube rest of bread and scatter over top. Pour melted butter over this. Bake at 325° for 1 hour, uncovered. This can be prepared 4 to 6 hours ahead or overnight in refrigerator.

CHICKEN BREASTS

6 boned chicken breasts
2 C. fresh bread crumbs
¾ C. Parmesan cheese
¼ C. parsley (chopped)

¼ tsp. garlic
2 tsp. salt
½ tsp. pepper
Melted butter

Dip boned chicken breasts in melted butter. Mix all other ingredients together and roll chicken breasts in mixture. Bake at 350° for 1 hour. If they brown too quickly, you may wish to cover the last 15-20 minutes. *I put the bread and parsley in a blender to crumb.

HAM PUFFS

16 slices bread (trim off crusts)
1 lb. chopped ham (2 C.)
1 lb. grated cheese (or 2 C. diced)
4 eggs

4 C. milk
½ tsp. dry mustard
½ tsp. pepper

Place 8 slices of bread in bottom of a greased 9 x 13-inch pan. Add ham and cheese; cover with remaining bread. Beat eggs; add milk, mustard and pepper. Pour over bread. Place in refrigerator overnight. Bake at 350° for 1 hour. You can use turkey or chicken instead of ham. Good for special breakfast or brunch. Serves 8.

DOUBLE COATED IOWA PORK CHOPS

6 Iowa pork chops
1 egg
¾ C. milk
¾ C. flour

3 T. melted oleo
1½ tsp. salt
¼ tsp. pepper
4 C. crushed rice cereal

Make a batter of egg, milk, flour, salt and pepper. Dip chops in batter, then roll in cereal crumbs. Arrange on shallow baking pan and drizzle with melted oleo. Bake at 350° for 1 hour. Makes 6 servings.

STUFFED PORK CHOPS

4 or 5 thick cut pork chops (Iowa cut)
1 pkg. Pepperidge farm dressing
½ C. finely chopped celery
½ C. finely chopped onion

¼ lb. butter or oleo
1 C. water
2 cans cream of chicken soup
1 can milk

Cut pockets in pork chop and brown in skillet. Saute celery and onion in butter until tender. Add to dressing and water. Fill pockets and put ½ of remaining dressing in bottom of 9 x 12-inch baking dish. Add stuffed pork chops. Put remainder of dressing on top. Mix 2 cans cream of chicken and 1 can milk to rinse out soup cans. Pour over and bake in slow oven 325° for 1½ hours.

DESSERTS

QUICK PEACH COBBLER

4 C. sliced fresh peaches (or apples)
1½ C. sugar
¾ C. flour
2 tsp. baking powder
¾ C. milk
¼ C. butter or oleo

Mix peaches with 1 C. sugar. Set oven at 350°. Put butter in 8 x 8-inch baking dish (or 8 x 12-inch dish). Set dish in oven to melt butter. Make batter of sugar, flour, baking powder and milk. Pour over melted butter. Do Not Stir. Pour peaches over batter. Do Not Stir. Bake 45 minutes.

JENKINS DESSERT

1 env. Knox gelatin (softened in ⅓ C. water)
½ C. sugar
2 egg yolks
¾ C. milk
1 tsp. vanilla
2 egg whites (beaten)
1 C. cream (whipped)
14 graham crackers (crushed)
3 T. powdered sugar
3 T. melted butter

Soften gelatin in cold water. Mix together sugar, egg yolks, milk and vanilla. Mix well and place over medium heat, stirring constantly and bring just to a boil and remove immediately from heat. Add gelatin and cool. Fold in beaten egg whites and whipped cream. Crush crackers with rolling pin. Add powdered sugar and melted butter to the crumbs; mix well. Place half of crumb mixture in bottom of baking dish. Pour gelatin mixture over crumbs and sprinkle remaining crumbs on top and chill.

ICE CREAM DESSERT

½ C. butter
⅔ C. brown sugar
1 C. coconut, flaked

2 C. Rice Chexs (crushed)
½ C. chopped nuts
½ gallon vanilla ice cream

Melt butter and sugar and bubble vigorously. Mix coconut, cereal and nuts together. Pour first mixture over second and stir until crumbly. Place half of it in bottom of 9 x 9-inch pan; slice ice cream and layer it over crumb mixture; place remaining crumb mixture over top; freeze. (Can do this recipe 1½ times for a 9 x 13-inch pan.)

APPLE CRISP

4 or 5 C. sliced apples
1 T. flour

½ C. sugar

TOPPING:
¾ C. brown sugar
⅓ C. butter
½ C. oatmeal
¾ C. flour

¼ tsp. soda
½ tsp. salt
1 tsp. cinnamon

Mix apples, flour and sugar together; place in an 8 x 8-inch baking dish. Mix together brown sugar, butter, flour, oatmeal, soda, salt and cinnamon and sprinkle over the apple mixture. Bake at 350° for 30 minutes or microwave on high setting for 16-18 minutes.

LUSCIOUS LAYERED BLUEBERRY DELIGHT

14 whole graham crackers
1 pkg. (6 servings size) instant vanilla
  pudding mix (prepared)

1 C. Cool Whip (thawed)
1 can blueberry pie filling

Line 9 x 9-inch square pan with whole graham crackers, breaking crackers if necessary. Prepare pudding mix as directed on package for pudding. Let stand 5 minutes, then blend in Cool Whip. Spread half of the pudding mixture over the crackers. Add another layer of crackers, top with remaining pudding mixture and remaining crackers. Spread pie filling over top layer of crackers. Chill 3 hours.

Need A Gift?

For

Shower • Birthday • Mother's Day • Anniversary • Christmas •

Turn Page for Order Form
(Order Now While Supply Lasts!)

TO ORDER COPIES OF

DIAL-A-DREAM
COOKBOOK

Please send me _____ copies of Dial-A-Dream at $11.95 each.

(Make checks payable to QUIXOTE PRESS.)

Name _____

Street _____

City _____ State _____ Zip Code _____

SEND ORDERS TO:

QUIXOTE PRESS
31798 K18S
Sioux City, IA 51109
800-571-BOOK

- -

TO ORDER COPIES OF

DIAL-A-DREAM
COOKBOOK

Please send me _____ copies of Dial-A-Dream at $11.95 each.

(Make checks payable to QUIXOTE PRESS.)

Name _____

Street _____

City _____ State _____ Zip Code _____

SEND ORDERS TO:

QUIXOTE PRESS
31798 K18S
Sioux City, IA 51109
800-571-BOOK

222

Since you have enjoyed this book, perhaps you would be interested in some of these others from QUIXOTE PRESS.

ARKANSAS BOOKS

HOW TO TALK ARKANSAS
    by Bruce Carlson .... paperback $7.95
ARKANSAS' ROADKILL COOKBOOK
    by Bruce Carlson .... paperback $7.95
REVENGE OF ROADKILL
    by Bruce Carlson .... paperback $7.95
GHOSTS OF THE OZARKS
    by Bruce Carlson .... paperback $9.95
A FIELD GUIDE TO SMALL ARKANSAS FEMALES
    by Bruce Carlson .... paperback $9.95
LET'S US GO DOWN TO THE RIVER 'N...
    by various authors .... paperback $9.95
ARKANSAS' VANISHING OUTHOUSE
    by Bruce Carlson .... paperback $9.95
TALL TALES OF THE MISSISSIPPI RIVER
    by Dan Titus .... paperback $9.95
LOST & BURIED TREASURE OF THE MISSISSIPPI RIVER
    by Netha Bell & Gary Scholl .... paperback $9.95
TALES OF HACKETT'S CREEK
    by Dan Titus .... paperback $9.95
UNSOLVED MYSTERIES OF THE MISSISSIPPI RIVER
    by Netha Bell .... paperback $9.95
101 WAYS TO USE A DEAD RIVER FLY
    by Bruce Carlson .... paperback $7.95
VACANT LOT, SCHOOL YARD & BACK ALLEY GAMES
    by various authors .... paperback $9.95
HOW TO TALK MIDWESTERN
    by Robert Thomas .... paperback $7.95
ARKANSAS COOKIN'
    by Bruce Carlson .... (3x5) paperback $5.95

DAKOTA BOOKS

HOW TO TALK DAKOTA .... paperback $7.95
Some Pretty Tame, but Kinda Funny Stories About Early
DAKOTA LADIES-OF-THE-EVENING
    by Bruce Carlson .... paperback $9.95

SOUTH DAKOTA ROADKILL COOKBOOK
by Bruce Carlson .... paperback $7.95
REVENGE OF ROADKILL
by Bruce Carlson .... paperback $7.95
101 WAYS TO USE A DEAD RIVER FLY
by Bruce Carlson .... paperback $7.95
LET'S US GO DOWN TO THE RIVER 'N...
by various authors .... paperback $9.95
LOST & BURIED TREASURE OF THE MISSOURI RIVER
by Netha Bell .... paperback $9.95
MAKIN' DO IN SOUTH DAKOTA
by various authors .... paperback $9.95
GUNSHOOTIN', WHISKEY DRINKIN', GIRL CHASIN' STORIES
OUT OF THE OLD DAKOTAS
by Netha Bell .... paperback $9.95
THE DAKOTAS' VANISHING OUTHOUSE
by Bruce Carlson .... paperback $9.95
VACANT LOT, SCHOOL YARD & BACK ALLEY GAMES
by various authors .... paperback $9.95
HOW TO TALK MIDWESTERN
by Robert Thomas .... paperback $7.95
DAKOTA COOKIN'
by Bruce Carlson .... (3x5) paperback $5.95

ILLINOIS BOOKS

ILLINOIS COOKIN'
by Bruce Carlson .... (3x5) paperback $5.95
THE VANISHING OUTHOUSE OF ILLINOIS
by Bruce Carlson .... paperback $9.95
A FIELD GUIDE TO ILLINOIS' CRITTERS
by Bruce Carlson .... paperback $7.95
YOU KNOW YOU'RE IN ILLINOIS WHEN...
by Bruce Carlson .... paperback $7.95
Some Pretty Tame, but Kinda Funny Stories About Early
ILLINOIS LADIES-OF-THE-EVENING
by Bruce Carlson .... paperback $9.95
ILLINOIS' ROADKILL COOKBOOK
by Bruce Carlson .... paperback $7.95
101 WAYS TO USE A DEAD RIVER FLY
by Bruce Carlson .... paperback $7.95

HOW TO TALK ILLINOIS
  by Netha Bell .... paperback $7.95
TALL TALES OF THE MISSISSIPPI RIVER
  by Dan Titus .... paperback $9.95
TALES OF HACKETT'S CREEK
  by Dan Titus .... paperback $9.95
UNSOLVED MYSTERIES OF THE MISSISSIPPI
  by Netha Bell .... paperback $9.95
LOST & BURIED TREASURE OF THE MISSISSIPPI RIVER
  by Netha Bell & Gary Scholl .... paperback $9.95
STRANGE FOLKS ALONG THE MISSISSIPPI
  by Pat Wallace .... paperback $9.95
LET'S US GO DOWN TO THE RIVER 'N...
  by various authors .... paperback $9.95
MISSISSIPPI RIVER PO' FOLK
  by Pat Wallace .... paperback $9.95
GHOSTS OF THE MISSISSIPPI RIVER (from Keokuk to St. Louis)
  by Bruce Carlson .... paperback $9.95
GHOSTS OF THE MISSISSIPPI RIVER (from Dubuque to Keokuk)
  by Bruce Carlson .... paperback $9.95
MAKIN' DO IN ILLINOIS
  by various authors .... paperback $9.95
MY VERY FIRST
  by various authors .... paperback $9.95
VACANT LOT, SCHOOL YARD & BACK ALLEY GAMES
  by various authors .... paperback $9.95
HOW TO TALK MIDWESTERN
  by Robert Thomas .... paperback $7.95

INDIANA BOOKS

HOW TO TALK INDIANA .... paperback $7.95
INDIANA'S ROADKILL COOKBOOK
  by Bruce Carlson .... paperback $7.95
REVENGE OF ROADKILL
  by Bruce Carlson .... paperback $7.95
A FIELD GUIDE TO SMALL INDIANA FEMALES
  by Bruce Carlson .... paperback $9.95
GHOSTS OF THE OHIO RIVER (from Cincinnati to Louisville)
  by Bruce Carlson .... paperback $9.95
LET'S US GO DOWN TO THE RIVER 'N...
  by various authors .... paperback $9.95

101 WAYS TO USE A DEAD RIVER FLY
by Bruce Carlson .... paperback $7.95
INDIANA'S VARNISHING OUTHOUSE
by Bruce Carlson .... paperback $9.95
VACANT LOT, SCHOOL YARD & BACK ALLEY GAMES
by various authors .... paperback $9.95
HOW TO TALK MIDWESTERN
by Robert Thomas .... paperback $7.95

IOWA BOOKS

IOWA COOKIN'
by Bruce Carlson .... (3x5) paperback $5.95
IOWA'S ROADKILL COOKBOOK
By Bruce Carlson .... paperback $7.95
REVENGE OF ROADKILL
by Bruce Carlson .... paperback $7.95
IOWA'S OLD SCHOOLHOUSES
by Carole Turner Johnston .... paperback $9.95
GHOSTS OF THE AMANA COLONIES
by Lori Erickson .... paperback $9.95
GHOSTS OF THE IOWA GREAT LAKES
by Bruce Carlson .... paperback $9.95
GHOSTS OF THE MISSISSIPPI RIVER (from Dubuque to Keokuk)
by Bruce Carlson .... paperback $9.95
GHOSTS OF THE MISSISSIPPI RIVER (from Minneapolis to Dubuque)
by Bruce Carlson .... paperback $9.95
GHOSTS OF POLK COUNTY, IOWA
by Tom Welch .... paperback $9.95
TALES OF HACKETT'S CREEK
by Dan Titus .... paperback $9.95
ME 'N WESLEY (stories about the homemade toys that
Iowa farm children made and played with around the turn of the century)
by Bruce Carlson .... paperback $9.95
TALL TALES OF THE MISSISSIPPI RIVER
by Dan Titus .... paperback $9.95
HOW TO TALK IOWA .... paperback $7.95
UNSOLVED MYSTERIES OF THE MISSISSIPPI
by Netha Bell .... paperback $9.95
101 WAYS TO USE A DEAD RIVER FLY
by Bruce Carlson .... paperback $7.95

LET'S US GO DOWN TO THE RIVER 'N...
 by various authors .... paperback $9.95
TRICKS WE PLAYED IN IOWA
 by various authors .... paperback $9.95
IOWA, THE LAND BETWEEN THE VOWELS
 (farm boy stories from the early 1900s)
 by Bruce Carlson .... paperback $9.95
LOST & BURIED TREASURE OF THE MISSISSIPPI RIVER
 by Netha Bell & Gary Scholl .... paperback $9.95
Some Pretty Tame, but Kinda Funny Stories About Early
IOWA LADIES-OF-THE-EVENING
 by Bruce Carlson .... paperback $9.95
THE VANISHING OUTHOUSE OF IOWA
 by Bruce Carlson .... paperback $9.95
IOWA'S EARLY HOME REMEDIES
 by 26 students at Wapello Elem. School .... paperback $9.95
IOWA - A JOURNEY IN A PROMISED LAND
 by Kathy Yoder .... paperback $16.95
LOST & BURIED TREASURE OF THE MISSOURI RIVER
 by Netha Bell .... paperback $9.95
FIELD GUIDE TO IOWA'S CRITTERS
 by Bruce Carlson .... paperback $7.95
OLD IOWA HOUSES, YOUNG LOVES
 by Bruce Carlson .... paperback $9.95
SKUNK RIVER ANTHOLOGY
 by Gene Olson .... paperback $9.95
VACANT LOT, SCHOOL YARD & BACK ALLEY GAMES
 by various authors .... paperback $9.95
HOW TO TALK MIDWESTERN
 by Robert Thomas .... paperback $7.95

KANSAS BOOKS

HOW TO TALK KANSAS .... paperback $7.95
STOPOVER IN KANSAS
 by Jon McAlpin .... paperback $9.95
LET'S US GO DOWN TO THE RIVER 'N ...
 by various authors .... paperback $9.95
LOST & BURIED TREASURE OF THE MISSOURI RIVER
 by Netha Bell .... paperback $9.95

101 WAYS TO USE A DEAD RIVER FLY
　　　by Bruce Carlson .... paperback $7.95
VACANT LOT, SCHOOL YARD & BACK ALLEY GAMES
　　　by various authors .... paperback $9.95
HOW TO TALK MIDWESTERN
　　　by Robert Thomas .... paperback $7.95

KENTUCKY BOOKS

GHOSTS OF THE OHIO RIVER (from Pittsburgh to Cincinnati)
　　　by Bruce Carlson .... paperback $9.95
GHOSTS OF THE OHIO RIVER (from Cincinnati to Louisville)
　　　by Bruce Carlson .... paperback $9.95
TALES OF HACKETT'S CREEK
　　　by Dan Titus .... paperback $9.95
LOST & BURIED TREASURE OF THE MISSISSIPPI RIVER
　　　by Netha Bell & Gary Scholl .... paperback $9.95
LET'S US GO DOWN TO THE RIVER 'N ...
　　　by various authors .... paperback $9.95
UNSOLVED MYSTERIES OF THE MISSISSIPPI
　　　by Netha Bell .... paperback $9.95
101 WAYS TO USE A DEAD RIVER FLY
　　　by Bruce Carlson .... paperback $7.95
TALL TALES OF THE MISSISSIPPI RIVER
　　　by Dan Titus .... paperback $9.95
MY VERY FIRST
　　　by various authors .... paperback $9.95
VACANT LOT, SCHOOL YARD & BACK ALLEY GAMES
　　　by various authors .... paperback $9.95

MICHIGAN BOOKS

MICHIGAN COOKIN'
　　　by Bruce Carlson .... (3x5) paperback $5.95
MICHIGAN'S ROADKILL COOKBOOK
　　　by Bruce Carlson .... paperback $7.95
MICHIGAN'S VANISHING OUTHOUSE
　　　by Bruce Carlson .... paperback $9.95

MINNESOTA BOOKS

MINNESOTA'S ROADKILL COOKBOOK
    by Bruce Carlson .... paperback $7.95
REVENGE OF ROADKILL
    by Bruce Carlson .... paperback $7.95
A FIELD GUIDE TO SMALL MINNESOTA FEMALES
    by Bruce Carlson .... paperback $9.95
GHOSTS OF THE MISSISSIPPI RIVER (from Minneapolis to Dubuque)
    by Bruce Carlson .... paperback $9.95
LAKES COUNTRY COOKBOOK
    by Bruce Carlson .... paperback $11.95
UNSOLVED MYSTERIES OF THE MISSISSIPPI
    by Netha Bell .... paperback $9.95
TALES OF HACKETT'S CREEK
    by Dan Titus .... paperback $9.95
GHOSTS OF SOUTHWEST MINNESOTA
    by Ruth Hein .... paperback $9.95
HOW TO TALK LIKE A MINNESOTA NATIVE .... paperback $7.95
MINNESOTA'S VANISHING OUTHOUSE
    by Bruce Carlson .... paperback $9.95
TALL TALES OF THE MISSISSIPPI RIVER
    by Dan Titus .... paperback $9.95
Some Pretty Tame, but Kinda Funny Stories About Early
MINNESOTA LADIES-OF-THE-EVENING
    by Bruce Carlson .... paperback $9.95
101 WAYS TO USE A DEAD RIVER FLY .... paperback $7.95
LOST & BURIED TREASURE OF THE MISSISSIPPI RIVER
    by Netha Bell & Gary Scholl .... paperback $9.95
VACANT LOT, SCHOOL YARD & BACK ALLEY GAMES
    · by various authors .... paperback $9.95
HOW TO TALK MIDWESTERN
    by Robert Thomas .... paperback $7.95
MINNESOTA COOKIN'
    by Bruce Carlson .... (3x5) paperback $5.95

MISSOURI BOOKS

MISSOURI COOKIN'
    by Bruce Carlson .... (3x5) paperback $5.95
MISSOURI'S ROADKILL COOKBOOK
    by Bruce Carlson .... paperback $7.95

REVENGE OF ROADKILL
by Bruce Carlson .... paperback $7.95
LET'S US GO DOWN TO THE RIVER 'N ...
by various authors .... paperback $9.95
LAKES COUNTRY COOKBOOK
by Bruce Carlson .... paperback $11.95
101 WAYS TO USE A DEAD RIVER FLY
by Bruce Carlson .... paperback $7.95
TALL TALES OF THE MISSISSIPPI RIVER
by Dan Titus .... paperback $9.95
TALES OF HACKETT'S CREEK
by Dan Titus .... paperback $9.95
STRANGE FOLKS ALONG THE MISSISSIPPI
by Pat Wallace .... paperback $9.95
LOST & BURIED TREASURE OF THE MISSOURI RIVER
by Netha Bell .... paperback $9.95
HOW TO TALK MISSOURIAN
by Bruce Carlson .... paperback $7.95
VACANT LOT, SCHOOL YARD & BACK ALLEY GAMES
by various authors .... paperback $9.95
HOW TO TALK MIDWESTERN
by Robert Thomas .... paperback $7.95
UNSOLVED MYSTERIES OF THE MISSISSIPPI
by Netha Bell .... paperback $9.95
LOST & BURIED TREASURE OF THE MISSISSIPPI RIVER
by Netha Bell & Gary Scholl .... paperback $9.95
MISSISSIPPI RIVER PO' FOLK
by Pat Wallace .... paperback $9.95
Some Pretty Tame, but Kinda Funny Stories About Early
MISSOURI LADIES-OF-THE-EVENING
by Bruce Carlson .... paperback $9.95
GUNSHOOTIN', WHISKEY DRINKIN', GIRL CHASIN'
STORIES OUT OF THE OLD MISSOURI TERRITORY
by Bruce Carlson .... paperback $9.95
THE VANISHING OUTHOUSE OF MISSOURI
by Bruce Carlson .... paperback $9.95
A FIELD GUIDE TO MISSOURI'S CRITTERS
by Bruce Carlson .... paperback $7.95
EARLY MISSOURI HOME REMEDIES
by various authors .... paperback $9.95
GHOSTS OF THE OZARKS
by Bruce Carlson .... paperback $9.95

MISSISSIPPI RIVER COOKIN' BOOK
    by Bruce Carlson .... paperback $11.95
MISSOURI'S OLD HOUSES, AND NEW LOVES
    by Bruce Carlson .... paperback $9.95
UNDERGROUND MISSOURI
    by Bruce Carlson .... paperback $9.95

NEBRASKA BOOKS

LOST & BURIED TREASURE OF THE MISSOURI RIVER
    by Netha Bell .... paperback $9.95
101 WAYS TO USE A DEAD RIVER FLY
    by Bruce Carlson .... paperback $7.95
LET'S US GO DOWN TO THE RIVER 'N ...
    by various authors .... paperback $9.95
HOW TO TALK MIDWESTERN
    by Robert Thomas .... paperback $7.95
VACANT LOT, SCHOOL YARD & BACK ALLEY GAMES
    by various authors .... paperback $9.95

TENNESSEE BOOKS

TALES OF HACKETT'S CREED
    by Dan Titus .... paperback $9.95
TALL TALES OF THE MISSISSIPPI RIVER
    by Dan Titus .... paperback $9.95
UNSOLVED MYSTERIES OF THE MISSISSIPPI
    by Netha Bell .... paperback $9.95
LOST & BURIED TREASURE OF THE MISSISSIPPI RIVER
    by Netha Bell & Gary Scholl .... paperback $9.95
LET'S US GO DOWN TO THE RIVER 'N ...
    by various authors .... paperback $9.95
101 WAYS TO USE A DEAD RIVER FLY
    by Bruce Carlson .... paperback $7.95
VACANT LOT, SCHOOL YARD & BACK ALLEY GAMES
    by various authors .... paperback $9.95

WISCONSIN BOOKS

HOW TO TALK WISCONSIN .... paperback $7.95
WISCONSIN COOKIN'
    by Bruce Carlson .... (3x5) paperback $5.95
WISCONSIN'S ROADKILL COOKBOOK
    by Bruce Carlson .... paperback $7.95
REVENGE OF ROADKILL
    by Bruce Carlson .... paperback $7.95
TALL TALES OF THE MISSISSIPPI RIVER
    by Dan Titus .... paperback $9.95
LAKES COUNTRY COOKBOOK
    by Bruce Carlson .... paperback $11.95
TALES OF HACKETT'S CREEK
    by Dan Titus .... paperback $9.95
LET'S US GO DOWN TO THE RIVER 'N ...
    by various authors .... paperback $9.95
101 WAYS TO USE A DEAD RIVER FLY
    by Bruce Carlson .... paperback $7.95
UNSOLVED MYSTERIES OF THE MISSISSIPPI
    by Netha Bell .... paperback $9.95
LOST & BURIED TREASURE OF THE MISSISSIPPI RIVER
    by Netha Bell & Gary Scholl .... paperback $9.95
GHOSTS OF THE MISSISSIPPI RIVER (from Dubuque to Keokuk)
    by Bruce Carlson .... paperback $9.95
HOW TO TALK MIDWESTERN
    by Robert Thomas .... paperback $7.95
VACANT LOT, SCHOOL YARD & BACK ALLEY GAMES
    by various authors .... paperback $9.95
MY VERY FIRST
    by various authors .... paperback $9.95
EARLY WISCONSIN HOME REMEDIES
    by various authors .... paperback $9.95
GHOSTS OF THE MISSISSIPPI RIVER (from Minneapolis to Dubuque)
    by Bruce Carlson .... paperback $9.95
THE VANISHING OUTHOUSE OF WISCONSIN
    by Bruce Carlson .... paperback $9.95
GHOSTS OF DOOR COUNTY, WISCONSIN
    by Geri Rider .... paperback $9.95
Some Pretty Tame, but Kinda Funny Stories About Early
WISCONSIN LADIES-OF-THE-EVENING
    by Bruce Carlson .... paperback $9.95

MIDWESTERN BOOKS

A FIELD GUIDE TO THE MIDWEST'S WORST RESTAURANTS
 by Bruce Carlson .... paperback $5.95
THE MOTORIST'S FIELD GUIDE TO MIDWESTERN FARM
EQUIPMENT (misguided information as only a city slicker can give it)
 by Bruce Carlson .... paperback $5.95
VACANT LOT, SCHOOL YARD & BACK ALLEY GAMES
OF THE MIDWEST YEARS AGO
 by various authors .... paperback $9.95
MIDWEST SMALL TOWN COOKING
 by Bruce Carlson .... (3x5) paperback $5.95
HITCHHIKING THE UPPER MIDWEST
 by Bruce Carlson .... paperback $7.95
101 WAYS FOR MIDWESTERNERS TO "DO IN" THEIR
NEIGHBOR'S PESKY DOG WITHOUT GETTING CAUGHT
 by Bruce Carlson .... paperback $5.95

RIVER BOOKS

ON THE SHOULDERS OF A GIANT
 by M. Cody and D. Walker .... paperback $9.95
SKUNK RIVER ANTHOLOGY
 by Gene "Will" Olson .... paperback $9.95
JACK KING vs. DETECTIVE MACKENZIE
 by Netha Bell .... paperback $9.95
LOST & BURIED TREASURES ALONG THE MISSISSIPPI
 by Netha Bell & Gary Scholl .... paperback $9.95
MISSISSIPPI RIVER PO' FOLK
 by Pat Wallace .... paperback $9.95
STRANGE FOLKS ALONG THE MISSISSIPPI
 by Pat Wallace .... paperback $9.95
GHOSTS OF THE OHIO RIVER (from Pittsburgh to Cincinnati)
 by Bruce Carlson .... paperback $9.95
GHOSTS OF THE OHIO RIVER (from Cincinnati to Louisville)
 by Bruce Carlson .... paperback $9.95
GHOSTS OF THE MISSISSIPPI RIVER (Minneapolis to Dubuque)
 by Bruce Carlson .... paperback $9.95
GHOSTS OF THE MISSISSIPPI RIVER (Dubuque to Keokuk)
 by Bruce Carlson .... paperback $9.95
TALL TALES OF THE MISSISSIPPI RIVER
 by Dan Titus .... paperback $9.95

TALL TALES OF THE MISSOURI RIVER
by Dan Titus .... paperback $9.95
RIVER SHARKS & SHENANIGANS
(tales of riverboat gambling of years ago)
by Netha Bell .... paperback $9.95
UNSOLVED MYSTERIES OF THE MISSISSIPPI
by Netha Bell .... paperback $9.95
TALES OF HACKETT'S CREEK (1940s Mississippi River kids)
by Dan Titus .... paperback $9.95
101 WAYS TO USE A DEAD RIVER FLY
by Bruce Carlson .... paperback $7.95
LET'S US GO DOWN TO THE RIVER 'N ...
by various authors .... paperback $9.95
LOST & BURIED TREASURE OF THE MISSOURI
by Netha Bell .... paperback $9.95

COOKBOOKS

ROARING 20's COOKBOOK
by Bruce Carlson .... paperback $11.95
DEPRESSION COOKBOOK
by Bruce Carlson .... paperback $11.95
LAKES COUNTRY COOKBOOK
by Bruce Carlson .... paperback $11.95
A COOKBOOK FOR THEM WHAT AIN'T DONE A LOT OF COOKIN'
by Bruce Carlson .... paperback $11.95
FLAT-OUT DIRT-CHEAP COOKIN' COOKBOOK
by Bruce Carlson .... paperback $11.95
APHRODISIAC COOKING
by Bruce Carlson .... paperback $11.95
WILD CRITTER COOKBOOK
by Bruce Carlson .... paperback $11.95
I GOT FUNNIER-THINGS-TO-DO-THAN-COOKIN' COOKBOOK
by Louise Lum .... paperback $11.95
MISSISSIPPI RIVER COOKIN' BOOK
by Bruce Carlson .... paperback $11.95
HUNTING IN THE NUDE COOKBOOK
by Bruce Carlson .... paperback $9.95
DAKOTA COOKIN'
by Bruce Carlson .... (3x5) paperback $5.95
IOWA COOKIN'
by Bruce Carlson .... (3x5) paperback $5.95

MICHIGAN COOKIN'
by Bruce Carlson .... (3x5) paperback $5.95
MINNESOTA COOKIN'
by Bruce Carlson .... (3x5) paperback $5.95
MISSOURI COOKIN'
by Bruce Carlson .... (3x5) paperback $5.95
ILLINOIS COOKIN'
by Bruce Carlson .... (3x5) paperback $5.95
WISCONSIN COOKIN'
by Bruce Carlson .... (3x5) paperback $5.95
HILL COUNTRY COOKIN'
by Bruce Carlson .... (3x5) paperback $5.95
MIDWEST SMALL TOWN COOKIN'
by Bruce Carlson .... (3x5) paperback $5.95
APHRODISIAC COOKIN'
by Bruce Carlson .... (3x5) paperback $5.95
PREGNANT LADY COOKIN'
by Bruce Carlson .... (3x5) paperback $5.95
GOOD COOKIN' FROM THE PLAIN PEOPLE
by Bruce Carlson .... (3x5) paperback $5.95
WORKING GIRL COOKING
by Bruce Carlson .... (3x5) paperback $5.95
COOKING FOR ONE
by Barb Layton .... paperback $11.95
SUPER SIMPLE COOKING
by Barb Layton .... (3x5) paperback $5.95
OFF TO COLLEGE COOKBOOK
by Barb Layton .... (3x5) paperback $5.95
COOKING WITH THINGS THAT GO SPLASH
by Bruce Carlson .... (3x5) paperback $5.95
COOKING WITH THINGS THAT GO MOO
by Bruce Carlson .... (3x5) paperback $5.95
COOKING WITH SPIRITS
by Bruce Carlson .... (3x5) paperback $5.95
INDIAN COOKING COOKBOOK
by Bruce Carlson .... paperback $9.95
DIAL-A-DREAM COOKBOOK
by Bruce Carlson .... (3x5) paperback $5.95
HORMONE HELPER COOKBOOK .... (3x5) paperback $5.95

MISCELLANEOUS BOOKS

DEAR TABBY (letters to and from a feline advice columnist)
by Bruce Carlson .... paperback $5.95
HOW TO BEHAVE (etiquette advice for non-traditional
and awkward circumstances such as attending dogfights,
what to do when your blind date turns out to be your spouse, etc.)
by Bruce Carlson .... paperback $5.95
REVENGE OF THE ROADKILL
by Bruce Carlson .... paperback $7.95